HAUNTED
LIVERPOOL 6

For Harold and Christine Helen Wilson

© Tom Slemen 2002

Published by The Bluecoat Press, Liverpool
Book design by March Design, Liverpool
Printed by The Universities Press (Belfast) Ltd

ISBN 1872568 90 4

Tom Slemen
HAUNTED
LIVERPOOL 6

The Bluecoat Press

Contents

Introduction

Welcome to the sixth volume of *Haunted Liverpool* in which you will read of various paranormal incidents that have taken place in the North West, and beyond, because in this age of the Internet, my tales have been featured on many websites, and so my readership now includes people from across the globe. In a single day I can receive over a hundred emails from people using the world-wide web: a homesick ex-pat Scouser living in Australia relating a ghostly tale of his old house on Scotland Road, a schoolgirl in California who wants to know if she is possessed, a Japanese Beatles fanatic who is intrigued by the Penny Lane Poltergeist, or John Lennon's obsession with the number nine, and so on.

It sounds such a cliché, but the Internet really has turned the world into a global village, and it is gratifying to find that people all over this planet – from Hollywood to Halewood – love a good ghost story. The fascination with what lies beyond the vague boundaries of our present knowledge is universal. Many of the emails I receive relate to premonitions which readers have experienced of future events. Some of these predictions have not yet come to pass, and some have turned out to be nothing more than nightmares – but a few prophecies of doom have indeed taken place.

I once received an email from a man named Gerald in Upton, telling me he had been having the same recurring bad dream about a car crash on a certain stretch of road in Liverpool. Days later, the crash took place at the precise location he had seen in his nightmares. Even the colour and model of the car involved was correct. On another occasion, a listener to my slot on the *Billy Butler Show* telephoned the studio to tell me of two plane crashes she had foreseen. One vision of a plane crashing into the Mersey came to her while she was awake, whilst another premonition of a jet landing in flames at Liverpool John Lennon Airport, was experienced vividly when she was asleep. Both prophesied events came to pass, just as she had described them. The crew and passengers of the plane that crashed into the River Mersey perished, while the people on board the jet that crash-landed onto the runway at the airport, survived.

The strangest, and probably the most grisly premonition ever related to me by a radio listener, came from a woman called Joan. She had suffered from insomnia throughout August 2001, and had decided to read in bed in the hope of eventually dropping off. Unfortunately she decided to read *Haunted Liverpool 2*, which her nephew had left at the house, and she became so engrossed in the paranormal tales, that she was still reading when the dawn light came creeping through the bedroom curtains.

On the following night, Joan managed to get a few hours sleep, but woke in a cold sweat after suffering a dreadful nightmare. In the dream, she found a pair of severed hands that were bound together with plastic strips. The hands were definitely female, and the nails were varnished with red nail polish. As she gingerly lifted the hands, she saw the red tissue and bone at the wrist stumps and screamed herself awake. The very same dream, in all its gory detail, replayed in Joan's sleeping mind following night. I will reveal the meaning of Joan's nightmares later on in this introduction.

In June 2001, a 30-year-old woman from Chorley named Valerie Clarke was invited onto BBC TV's *Kilroy* show because of her alleged psychic powers. Valerie told presenter Robert Kilroy Silk that she had had a terrifying nightmare about a massive explosion caused by a plane crashing into one of the Twin Towers of the World Trade Center in Manhattan. The catastrophic image of the crash haunted the Lancashire housewife, who had experienced premonitions in dreams before. Kilroy Silk nodded and moved on to the other guests to hear of less dramatic predictions. After the show, Valerie's grim tale of precognition was quickly forgotten.

Three months later, on the morning of 11 September, the skies over New York were clear and blue, and the temperature was an agreeable 70 degrees. One TV weather forecaster said it was 'a perfect day – too good to be true'. Meanwhile, a Boeing 767 from Boston – American Airlines Flight 11 – bound for Los Angeles with 81 passengers on board, quickly attracted the attention of air traffic controllers. The plane left the runway at 7:59am and headed west, over the Adirondacks, before taking a sudden unexpected turn south. Flight 11 slanted down towards New York city.

Meanwhile, American Flight 757 had left Dulles; United Flight 175 left Boston at 7:58am, and United Flight 93 left Newark three minutes later, bound for San Francisco. The planes climbed gracefully into clear azure skies, all on transcontinental flights, laden with highly-inflammable fuel, on this perfect – too good to be true – warm autumn day.

At 8.45am, one of the planes slammed into the World Trade Center's north tower. Office workers on the 96th floor watched in horror and disbelief through plate-glass windows as the manned missile of doom came to take their lives. People scrambled for the elevators in vain, while others did not even have time to rush from their desks. The thousands of people in the floors above were as good as dead from that moment.

The plane ripped through the skyscraper's outer skin and parts of the aircraft – and numerous bodies – exploded from the other side of the building. A gruesome rain of glass, steel, high-octane fuel, office furniture and burning bodies began a slow motion fall onto the streets of Manhattan, one thousand feet below. The bewildered people of New York heard the sonic boom and looked skywards to the twin cathedrals of capitalism. Most surmised that it had been a terrible accident. Perhaps the pilot had lost altitude through engine failure and had been attempting to ditch the full tanks of aviation fuel into the river. The thought of terrorism never entered most people's minds at the time of the first crash. The flaming tyre of the aircraft wheel thudded into the street; then came a leg, a hand, a torso in charred clothing with a necktie fluttering. New Yorkers prayed and wept for the victims of the tragic 'accident', as a blizzard of documents and papers followed them down.

The ruptured tanks of jet fuel incinerated everyone and everything from the 96th to the 103rd floors. The searing river of fire gushed into elevator shafts to spread its destruction downwards and upwards. Sirens wailed across the city as police and paramedics rushed to the scene of the unfolding disaster. People poured out of the north tower with appalling injuries; most were in shock. Many were burnt from head to toe. Of the first six patients admitted into an ambulance, two died on the way to St Vincent's Hospital.

United Flight 175, which had left Boston at 7.58am, bound for Los Angeles, had made a bizarre 30-degree turn, followed by an even sharper one before it hurtled down on Manhattan, to smash into the 87th floor of the south tower at 9.06am. By now, every camera in the metropolis was trained on the towers, as were the eyes of the crowds in the street and millions of people incredulously watching television screens around the world.

Once again, people were among the falling debris, and now, the horrified onlookers were realising that this was no accident. It had to be terrorism. The worst was yet to come. On that fateful day, the world watched as both towers collapsed in turn and thousands of people trapped in the buildings were literally vapourised in the final stages of the tragedy. My abiding memory of that day is the sight of the couple who jumped to their deaths holding hands. There was further loss of life at the Pentagon and in Pennsylvania, where the other two hijacked planes crashed.

The world was stunned by the terrorist attacks on America. In England, Valerie Clarke, the Lancashire psychic who had described her nightmare about a plane crashing into the north tower on *Kilroy*, said that her blood turned turned to ice when she saw the televised news of the attacks.

Joan, the listener to the *Billy Butler Show* who had dreamt of the severed hands, also received a shock, weeks after the terrorist attacks. Her son, James, telephoned her from New York and said that the police had made a grisly discovery on the roof of the building he had been evacuated from in Manhattan, close to the World Trade Center. They had found the bound-up hands of the stewardess from Flight 11. The hands had been tied together by the terrorists with plastic strips and must have been severed in the explosion.

Perhaps one day, when premonitions are taken more seriously, we could have a 'Premonition Bureau' where people could have their predictions catalogued, maybe with a view to preventing tragedies that have been foreseen.

The attacks on the World Trade Center were a chilling wake-up call to those of us who were complacent about our fragile mortality, but it saddens me to think that perhaps thousands of people could have been saved had we known a lot more about the nature of premonitions.

Tom Slemen

Through the Eyes of a Dead Woman

In around 1972 or 1973, Robert Moody, a 30-year-old Liverpool man, started getting stabbing pains in the back of his jaw. His mother persuaded him to go to the local dentist on Lawrence Road. The dentist x-rayed his jaw and discovered that he had impacted wisdom teeth. They would have to come out, or he would end up in continual agony. Robert Moody was terrified of needles, the smell of burning tooth enamel and the sight of blood, so the dentist decided to use gas. He assured his nervous patient that he would not hear or feel the crack of teeth while under the effects of the gas.

On a bright sunny afternoon, Robert Moody reluctantly sat back in the dentist's chair and took a deep breath. His hands and legs were trembling uncontrollably. The mask with the tube was gently applied to his face, and he thought, "I wonder if this will work?" Because he was one of those anxious insomniacs who lie in bed, wondering when, or if, they will reach the point when they will actually start falling asleep.

Desperately trying to subdue his rising panic, Moody inhaled the sickly gas and suddenly found himself somewhere else. He was in a familiar street, and the time of day looked like late afternoon. The street had rows of terraced houses with low walls and bay windows. At the bottom of the street was the wall of the cemetery on Smithdown Road. It suddenly came to him: "This is Cranbourne Road!"

Cranbourne Road was where his Auntie Maureen lived, on the border of Wavertree and Edge Hill, just around the corner from the dentist's. But the street looked all wrong somehow; the lampposts were old fashioned and so were the few cars parked on the road. Three girls and a little boy were playing with a skipping rope on the pavement, and they were chanting, "One, two, three alaira". The children lowered the rope to let Robert Moody past, and one of the girls called to the others, "Hey! Let this old woman past".

"Cheeky kid," Moody thought.

Then suddenly he realised that he had a headscarf on. He looked down and was disturbed to find that he was dressed in female clothing, but he kept on walking and before long he was automatically opening a small gate and walking to a front door. There was a number on this door which I will not reveal, because people are living at this house on Cranbourne Road and I do not want to alarm them.

When Robert Moody entered the house, he stopped in the hallway, and realised that he was suffering from amnesia of some sort. The only thing he was certain of was that his name was Alice and that he led a very lonely life. He studied his hands, they were old and wrinkled and felt alien to him, as if they belonged to somebody else. In trepidation he approached a mirror and gulped in panic at his reflection; staring back at him was a frail old woman, with a quizzical look on her face. Then he noticed a light shining through the mirror, as if it was a one-way mirror with someone shining a torch behind it.

Then he was flooded with a light as bright as the sun and in the distance he heard his dentist echo the words, "Some more," to the nurse. The nurse administered more gas. Moody was back in the gloomy old house in what seemed like the 1950s. This time he froze in horror as two men, aged about 25, burst into the room and started viciously attacking him. They punched him and kicked him and, totally unable to defend himself, he fell to the floor. As they continued kicking him he saw flashes of vivid blue light, and heard a loud, sickening crack. The agony was so intense that he cried out "God help me!" and then passed out.

Moody woke up with a start, and simultaneously sprang up from the reclined dentist's chair, butting the large circular light as he did so. The dentist and nurse grappled with him as he yelled hysterically, with blood trickling from his mouth. The dentist had successfully removed the impacted wisdom teeth, but Robert Moody's mouth was swollen and raw.

He gradually calmed down as the dentist gently asked him about the nightmare he had suffered. Moody related the horribly realistic dream he had experienced, and the nurse turned white when she heard it. She explained that when she was a child, she had lived on the road which Moody had dreamed about – Cranbourne Road. In the 1950s, an old spinster had been brutally murdered there, and the number of her house had been the very same number that Moody had seen on the door. All the children on the road knew about the murder and from that time onwards they had given the house a very wide berth. The victim's name was Mrs Rimmer, that was all the nurse could remember.

The whole episode made a very strong impression on poor Robert Moody and he decided to do a bit of research into the murder at the library. When he found out what Mrs Rimmer's first name had been, his insides churned over unpleasantly. Alice – her name was Alice Rimmer.

The two men charged with the brutal attack were named Burns and Devlin. They had been after Alice's life savings which she allegedly kept at the house. They were charged, tried, and later hanged for their crime. However, the men who carried out the attack in the dream were nothing like the pictures Moody found of Burns and Devlin, so he became convinced that the wrong men had been hanged. To this day Robert Moody is puzzled as to how gas at the dentist's managed to transport his mind back in time to a dreadful murder.

Guilty Conscience

In 1950, in the state of Texas, the police were urgently called to the home of a 70-year-old, George M Stafford. They found him lying in a large pool of blood, having been shot twice in the chest at point-blank range. The place had been ransacked, pointing to robbery as a probable motive. A macabre clue to the killer's identity needed no detective work, for the dead man, who was originally from Wallasey, had traced out the name 'DAN', in large wobbly letters, in his own blood, with his finger, just before he died.

The detectives studied the name written in blood and then mentally started to go through the names of known local criminals. They soon paid a visit to a poverty-stricken loser and petty thief named Dan Edwards, and discovered that he had indeed known Mr Stafford, whom he described as an eccentric old limey. Dan Edwards repeatedly insisted that he had had nothing to do with the old man's murder, but could not realistically explain to the police where he had managed to obtain $100 in cash, which was discovered when he was searched.

Edwards was arrested and charged with murder, but managed to get off on a technicality. He moved to another state out of feelings of guilt, and before long strange things started to happen to him. One night in a scruffy motel, Edwards was lying in bed asleep when something cold splashed on his face. He opened his eyes, but instead of the neon glow from the motel sign filtering through the blinds, he saw nothing but a redness, because blood was dripping into his eyes from the ceiling. Edwards stumbled out of bed and screamed for the manager. The manager heard the commotion and assumed that it was just another drunk making a nuisance of himself. He trudged across the parking lot from reception and flung open the door to Edwards' room, expecting trouble. Instead, he found the terrified guest pointing up at the ceiling, wiping his eyes which were covered in blood.

The manager looked up at the ceiling and he also saw the blood dripping from a scarlet patch on the ceiling. He tried to calm the hysterical man and helped him clean himself up and found him some clean sheets. Minutes later, when they again looked up at the ceiling, the red stain started to fade away as mysteriously as it had appeared. Within a short time, all trace of it had vanished.

The same gruesome phenomenon haunted Dan Edwards for the next fifteen months, and was witnessed by dozens of horrified people, including a newspaper reporter and a policeman. On one occasion, as he was enjoying some fast food in a diner, the imprint of a bloodstained hand suddenly appeared on the back of his jacket. On another occasion, Edwards was dating a woman, and as he went to pay for a meal in a restaurant, he found that the dollar notes in his wallet were soaked with sticky crimson blood.

In 1952, Edwards could stand it no longer and he put a pistol to his head and blew his brains out, to end his grisly persecution.

Born Too Late

Love can transcend almost any obstacle. It can leapfrog over age differences, it can see beyond the colour of a person's skin, and it can bridge the gulf between rich and poor. The following story, which happened a long time ago, seems to indicate that love can even transcend time itself.

On a snowy Saturday afternoon in December 1901, Mrs Rose Mooney sat basking in front of a blazing log fire in the caretaker's quarters at Speke Hall; a beautiful, half-timbered Tudor mansion in south Liverpool. Rose's husband, Desmond, looked after the hall with the help of a few gardeners and a stableman. On this wintry afternoon, he was in a pub in town, enjoying a drink with a relative. Mrs Mooney's only company was her 11-year-old daughter Maude, a beautiful little girl with long, deep auburn hair that she usually wore in two pony-tails. Mrs Mooney was five months pregnant, and little Maude was looking forward to having a baby brother or sister to look after. Anyway, on this Saturday afternoon, Maude went out to play in the beautifully-kept grounds of Speke Hall, as she did most days. Sometimes her cousin or a friend from school joined in the games, but being December and close to Christmas, all Maude's friends were spending their time with their families and relatives.

Maude decided to build a snowman, and even borrowed her father's old fishing hat to put on top of his big, round head. Around four o'clock that afternoon, twilight started to creep across the sky, so Mrs Mooney pulled a coat round her shoulders and went to shout for her daughter. There was no sign of her, not a sound in the silent frosty garden. When Mr Mooney returned home, he joined in the search.

Maude's worried parents followed the trail of footsteps leading from the snowman on the lawn in front of the house, for over two hundred yards, and then stopped in their tracks. There were unidentified footprints next to the impressions of Maude's shoes. They looked slightly larger than Maude's and seemed to have been made by shoes with a heel. The mystery deepened when the Mooneys discovered that both sets of footprints came to a full stop near two vast, sprawling 500-year-old yew trees, known as 'Adam and Eve'.

The gardener, George, came trotting across the lawn and breathlessly added another puzzle to the unfolding mystery. He said he had seen Maude throwing snowballs at what looked like a little girl, wearing a large floppy hat. Mr Mooney interrupted him, "No, George, that must have been the snowman with my hat on."

The gardener shook his head and insisted that a young girl, dressed in a peculiar black costume, had been playing with Maude – she had certainly not been a snowman by any stretch of the imagination. This new piece of information upset Mrs Mooney and she started to cry.

"Where on earth can she be?" she sobbed, as her equally bewildered and distraught husband put his arm round her and tried to comfort her.

"Don't worry pet, I'm sure she's OK," he said, trying to hide the anxiety in his voice. Then, turning to George, he said, "Take Mrs Mooney back to the house will you George? I'm just going to find out where Maude's hiding." Under his breath he added, "I'm going to ring the police."

Moments later, before George could do as he was asked, the sound of a child laughing could be heard coming from the trees. It was Maude's laughter. The lost child suddenly came running and skipping across the snow-covered lawns, wearing a little cape of some sort.

Her relieved parents and the gardener closed in on her and as her mother sobbed and hugged Maude, her father chided her and demanded to know where she had been. Maude's mood immediately changed. She dropped her head in a sulk and her bottom lip quivered.

"I'm not to say. It's a secret," she muttered, in a quiet voice.

"Secret?! I'll give you a damn good hiding my girl, never mind secret. Now tell us where you've been. Your Mum and I have been worried sick."

"Stop it, Desmond. She's alright, that's all that matters. She'll tell us what happened in her own time. Now let's get her inside before we all freeze to death!"

Rose Mooney, like any mother who has briefly faced the possibility of harm coming to her child, gratefully squeezed her daughter in her arms and led her indoors.

Despite her father's obvious anger and frustration, Maude could not be persuaded to say where she had been that afternoon. Desmond Mooney examined the little black cloak that had been found on his daughter. It was beautifully made of luxurious black velvet with a dark violet silk lining, decorated with a border of gold stitching. There were no labels on it to indicate who had made it or who its owner was.

On many more occasions, until August of the following year, Maude would vanish for hours on end, and her parents and many other people visiting the hall were a witness to the strange disappearances. Sometimes, a girl's voice and laughter could be heard, even though she could not be seen. On such occasions the gardener's old English sheepdog used to behave strangely, and seemed to be able to discern things in the grounds that humans could not.

In the end, Desmond Mooney secured a new job in Ormskirk, and he and his family moved away from Speke Hall. Maude Mooney cried her eyes out when they moved, as if she felt so intensely for her invisible playmate that she could not bear to part from him or her.

In 1911, when Maude reached the age of 21, she finally broke her silence, and told her mother about the circumstances of the supernatural goings-on at Speke Hall. She described how she had fallen in love with a little Cavalier boy named Tristam. He had lived hundreds of years ago, but could somehow visit the present now and then. How this had been possible Maude could not say, but what she did know was that she had loved Tristam, and he had returned her love. They would walk hand in hand through the grounds, laughing and playing, and she had even met his parents and their servants at the hall. They rode on Tristam's horse along the banks of the Mersey and kissed under one of the old yew trees. He had often played an instrument like a guitar and serenaded her, and gave her roses. He even gave her his cape when Maude was shivering with cold that December when they first met. The little lovers had even carved their initials on a tree.

The identity of Tristam has not been established as yet. It is said that in 1969, when Maude was a frail old woman, she asked to be taken to Speke Hall. There she passed away on a bright sunny afternoon, aged 79. Perhaps she has been reunited with Tristam for good now.

Change of Heart

In the mid-1950s, in Liverpool, a man named Leo Burns lost his wife. She died as she was undergoing an operation, and she was only 32. Leo was knocked sideways by the untimely death of his wife, and, like many men in such a position, he turned to drink. Within six months, he had lost his job and virtually all his friends. Sinking deeper and deeper into depression, he was eventually evicted for non-payment of rent and ended up as a vagrant.

The only real friend Leo had was an elderly priest who urged him to stop wallowing in self pity. The priest repeatedly encouraged Leo to get a job and to get his life back on track, but he continued to drink; he just could not see any light. He would beg and steal to get enough money for a bottle of gin or whisky, and often cadged food at the home for vagrants on Shaw Street.

In the bitter winter of December 1956, Leo struggled to sleep on a park bench wrapped in newspapers, but it was no good; the biting cold cut through the newspapers and his filthy, tattered clothes and seemed to gnaw at his bones. He trudged out of the park blowing his fingers and then thrusting them inside his coat pockets to try and get some sensation back. He was lucky enough to be given a bunk at a home for the destitute on Brownlow Hill, but had to leave after stealing a down-and-out man's suit while he was asleep. Leo had no plans to freeze to death sleeping under the stars, so he devised a plan to get good food and shelter. He picked up a brick from a back alley and hurled it through a jeweller's window on Mount Pleasant. He knew it would not be long before the police turned up to arrest him, and he thought to himself that they had delicious Christmas dinners at Walton Jail at this time of year!

Three policemen duly did turn up, and Leo stood on the pavement by the smashed window, ready to be handcuffed, but instead they ran past him and chased an innocent man trotting after a bus by the Adelphi

Hotel.

"It was me you idiots! Me!" he called after them.

The jeweller swore at Leo and told him to beat it.

With the temperature still dropping and a freezing wind whistling straight off the Mersey, Leo quickly devised another plan to get himself arrested and taken off the wintry streets. He walked into a restaurant on Bold Street which he and his wife used to frequent, wearing the stolen suit . A waiter escorted him to a table and offered him the menu. Before Leo made his choices, he asked for a cigar, which the restaurant offered freely to customers as a courtesy. He ordered the best wine, then, after studying the menu for some time – he was in no rush – he decided to try duck, a few exotic dishes and a dessert to follow. He would enjoy his meal, and the cosy, warm surroundings, before declaring himself insolvent. Once the proprietors found out that he could not pay the bill, they were bound to call the police who would arrest him and lock him up. That would earn him a few warm nights in Cheapside or Walton, just in time for the Christmas dinner.

Once again though, his criminal intentions backfired. Leo asked for the bill, read the amount due, then leaned back on the chair, puffing on the cigar.

"Can't pay I'm afraid," he smirked. "I'm stony broke."

The waiter turned red with anger, then signalled to a colleague, who kept the door covered in case Leo attempted to make a run for it. The manager was summoned. A small fat man, with a curly mop of silvery hair, emerged from the back of the restaurant. When he saw Leo, he reacted as if he had seen a ghost – as it turned out, the ghost of a much missed person. His face drained of colour and became expressionless.

"Daniel, is that – you?" he finally stammered.

Leo was baffled, this was not the reaction he had expected. His plan was going wrong again.

"Pardon?" he said.

The Jewish restaurant owner muttered something in Hebrew and seemed to recoil from him. Then tears started to roll down the old man's face as he stared intently at Leo, examining each of his features in turn. The two waiters looked on in complete puzzlement. The restaurant owner told Leo that he was the exact double of his younger brother Daniel, who had died in a German concentration camp in World War Two. The sobbing man reached out and grabbed Leo's hand and squeezed it hard.

Needless to say, when the waiters told their employer that Leo was just a penniless bum, the old man ignored them and Leo was let off without any punishment. The restaurant owner apologised to his customers as he wiped away the tears.

When Leo Burns thought about the fate of his double in Auschwitz, he finally saw the light. Nothing he had gone through was as bad as suffering the horrors of a concentration camp. This stark realisation quickly helped him to pull himself together, and within weeks he had found a job, and although it was a long battle, he finally kicked his drink habit. I suppose the moral of this story is that however bad things may seem, there is always someone worse off than yourself.

*

Incidentally, in the concentration camp at Jasenovac, on the night of 29 August 1942, orders were issued for executions. Bets were made as to who could liquidate the largest number of inmates. Peter Brzica cut the throats of 1,360 prisoners with a specially sharpened butcher's knife. Having been proclaimed the prize-winner of the hideous competition, he was elected King of the Cut-throats. A gold watch, silver service, and a roasted sucking pig and wine were his other rewards.

Jasenovac Concentration Camp distinguished itself because of the high proportion of young inmates sent there. In 1942 the camp held a staggering 24,000 youngsters, of whom twelve thousand were murdered in cold blood by the commandant.

Christmas Play

In the Scotland Road area, in the 1930s, there was a small firm which supplied materials to the building trade. The owner of this business was an elderly Irishman, George Donovan, a man reputed to be the living embodiment of Ebenezer Scrooge. Not only was he a skinflint, he was also a notorious taskmaster who forced his employees to work over the holidays – including Christmas.

A week before the Christmas of 1935, several bags of sand went missing from Mr Donovan's builder's yard, and the old snowy-haired Irishman was quick to accuse his employees of theft, but they all strenuously denied any knowledge of the whereabouts of the missing sand. The police were called in, and the mystery deepened when several residents in a street near Donovan's business also reported a number of bizarre thefts.

Stifling a grin under his walrus moustache, Police Constable Guthrie listened to the tearful account of one elderly resident named Lambert, who had been left emotionally devastated after discovering that the stuffed remains of his old cockatoo had been stolen from his parlour. The heartless thief had taken nothing else, which added an air of mystery to the incident. That same day, twenty-two chairs went missing from the Crescent Congregational Chapel in nearby Field Street. Six more chairs also unaccountably vanished from the furniture depository on Cazneau Street. PC Guthrie and two other policemen whose beats covered that area of Everton, also learned that a barmaid named Mrs Currivan had been aghast to find that her ankle-length coat had been stolen from under her nose in the Swan public house. The thief must have been swift and small, as he would have had to duck under the small hatchway in the bar counter to steal the coat, yet no one had seen a thing. An eyepatch belonging to Mr Jones, the one-eyed owner of the Swan, had also been taken, yet the agile looter had not stolen any spirits or cash from the till.

PC Guthrie and his colleagues gradually lost interest in these minor thefts, but old Mr Donovan went to the police station and demanded to know how the investigation into the theft of his sacks of sand was progressing, and the desk sergeant said that he would ask Guthrie when he returned from his beat. Donovan stormed off moodily, and outside, in the falling snow, he bumped into Constable Guthrie.

"Ah! Just the man I want to see. Have you found my merchandise yet constable?"

"Yes sir, I have," Guthrie replied.

"Oh! ... Well I'm glad to hear it! ... Who took it?" Donovan asked, somewhat taken aback.

"I'll show you, sir, if you'd just like to follow me," the policeman said with a wry smile, and he escorted the Irishman to a squalid slum, just a few streets away.

At the end of a narrow, dreary court, a crowd of poverty-stricken children and a few bemused mothers and fathers were gathered around a strange sight. A few children were standing on a 'desert island' made from Donovan's sand. One child wore a newspaper pirate hat, Mrs Currivan's ankle-length coat – which he had 'borrowed' from the barmaid – and he brandished a wooden sword. His ragamuffin friend held old Mr Lambert's stuffed cockatoo, and he kept squealing, "Pieces of eight!" A tiny pirate girl stood nearby wearing the eyepatch stolen from the manager of the Swan pub.

The audience of spellbound children and world-wearied parents sat on the chairs that had been reported stolen. It was a threadbare production of *Treasure Island* in the children's theatre of make-believe. The performance came to a heart-stopping standstill when the little actors saw PC Guthrie and Mr Donovan looking on, but the old Irishman, clearing his throat, suddenly said, "Go on, continue with the show, children," a quiver in his voice betraying the fact that he had been moved by the spectacle.

After the imaginary curtain came down, everyone clapped and whistled, and Mr Donovan bought every child an apple or orange. The children's innocent play, staged in a corner of a slum where Santa never ventured, had melted George Donovan's cynical heart.

Ghost of Clayton Square

The following strange story was related to me by a very down-to-earth couple in Allerton. I have interviewed them and taped their story.

In February 2000, Adam, a 30-year-old man from Speke, left the Virgin Megastore in town with his friend Tony. The day was Monday, 14 February, Valentine's Day, and Adam's girlfriend Allison had asked him to buy a romantic video and a little gift for her. Nothing extravagant, just a little thing that would mean a lot.

Adam searched the shelves in the store but could not find a suitable video. Tony, getting increasingly bored, suggested *Last Tango In Paris*, but Adam said there was nothing romantic about the film. So, the two young men wandered off into Clayton Square Shopping Centre and found themselves outside the Body Shop.

"Do us a favour, Tony," Adam said. "I get completely flustered when I go into shops like this. Go and get me a basket of smellies, will you? I'll buy you a pint."

"No way! You must be joking! I'm not doing your dirty work for you."

"Ah! Go on, Tony. I won't have anything to give to Allison and I promised."

"You need to get a grip, mate. That Allison's got you round her little finger. She's turning you into a middle-aged bore. You never go to the match any more and what's happened to our Saturday night benders?"

"But me and Allison are saving ..." Adam began.

"Leave it out, Adam. You can stuff your smellies and your romantic videos. I'm off," snarled Tony.

He marched off angrily, leaving Adam lingering around the Body Shop window. Suddenly, a voice behind him said: "Hello there". The stranger was about twenty at the most, and had a mullet hairstyle with a feathered fringe and a parting down the middle of his head. He wore a distinctive black V-necked pullover, and on which there was a logo of a pouncing cat, and underneath, the word 'Slazenger'. His jeans were baggy at the top, but tapered inwards as they went down to his 'Gola' trainers.

Adam nodded back, then walked into the Body Shop to get away from the strange, out-dated looking youth. But the youth followed him and said something which stopped Adam in his tracks: "I used to go with Allison Jones."

"What?" asked Adam, swinging round to face him.

"I saw you with her in the precinct the other day. She hasn't changed much."

"I'll mention you to her. What's your name?" Adam responded, unenthusiastically.

"Paul. Say Paul from High Park Street. Tell her I was asking," the youth replied.

"When were you seeing her?" Adam asked, not really enjoying this conversation with one of Allison's ex-boyfriends.

Paul said that he had gone out with Allison from when she was thirteen, until she was fifteen. As she was now twenty-six, this meant that he had dated her from 1987 to 1989, about twelve years ago. Adam felt dubious about this character asking his about Allison. He was surprised to find that he seemed to know everything about the girl's family, and her friends.

Suddenly Adam had what he thought was a bright idea. He asked Paul if he would go into the Body Shop and buy a gift for Allison. He admitted that he had a hang up about asking for feminine things in shops. Paul nodded amenably and went into the store. He soon came out with the basketful of lotions and creams.

Adam thanked him.

"How come you're not buying your girl something today? It's Valentine's Day you know," he asked.

Paul seemed choked up all of a sudden, and his eyes became watery. He simply shrugged and said nothing. Adam suspected that he was single, and had probably just come out of a relationship. He felt awkward, realising that he had been tactless. Trying to lighten the mood, he laughed and said to Paul, "She wanted me to get her a romantic video, but I couldn't find anything. I was thinking of getting her a 'Forever Friends' teddy bear, a big one. You could go in and get it for me if you want."

"She used to have a cabbage patch doll called Trudy," said Paul.

"Wait till I tell her all this, she'll go bright red," giggled Adam. "Trudy!"

"There were two films she loved. One was *ET*," Paul suggested.

"That's years old," Adam frowned.

"When ET used to say 'bee goood', then point to his heart and say, 'I'll be right here,' she always used to cry."

Unconvinced, Adam said, "Nah, she's seen that film about fifty times. What was the other video she liked?"

"An old black and white film. It was called *A Guy Named Joe*. It was about a pilot from the Second World War who died, but he comes back from heaven to help the boyfriend of the girl he left behind."

"I'm not getting her a black and white film, she'd go mad."

All of a sudden, Adam noticed that Paul was silently crying. Tears rolled down his cheeks. Before he could ask him what was wrong, the youth turned and walked away. He vanished round a corner and never returned. Adam searched for him, but could not find him anywhere.

When Adam went home to Allison, he told her about Paul from High Park Street, and she seemed to go numb with shock. She said he could not possibly have chatted with Paul, because he had been killed in a car crash in Widnes years ago – on Valentine's Day. Adam's stomach turned over when she told him this; she even produced an old photograph of Paul, and it was the same person he had spoken to in Clayton Square. Allison admitted that she did once have a cabbage patch doll named Trudy, and yes, she always cried at the end of *ET*. She also recalled that in her teenage days, her favourite romantic film had been *A Guy Named Joe*, so Adam managed to get a copy of the film and cradled an emotional Allison in his arms as they watched it.

The Crying Woman of the Dingle

In 2001, a psychical researcher who had looked into paranormal phenomenon for some 41 years, sadly passed away. His name was Tony Prince, and his wife gave me all his books, all his meticulous notes, and many of his audio and video tapes and photographs of a variety of phenomena ranging from UFOs to EVP (electronic voice phenomenon). One of the strange cases Tony Prince investigated was the 'Crying Woman of the Dingle' – a strange apparition that was said to be at large in a specific area of south Liverpool in the 1970s.

Tony Prince first heard about the banshee-like ghost while he was at the Irish Centre on Mount Pleasant one night. A group of women, including a hospital specialist, told Tony that the people in one part of the Dingle lived in fear of hearing the sounds of a crying woman, because those who had heard her cries, had either died within a week, or lost someone within days. Tony Prince had heard of such tales before, regarding the infamous banshee. A banshee is a ghostly female figure, dressed in black with long white hair. She is usually heard rather than seen, and she announces an imminent death by crying in the vicinity of the house where someone will pass away.

Tony Prince was very sceptical of banshees, but as time went on, he heard more and more about the Crying Woman of the Dingle. Tony's friend, a medical student called Alan, had remarked one day about three recent deaths in Dingle Lane, Ullet Road and Wellesley Road, which had occurred after people reported hearing a woman sobbing under a window, at all hours in the morning.

Tony Prince carefully made enquiries, and even spoke to the family of one man who had died in his sleep in Ullet Road, and they all related the same weird story about how a woman had been heard crying outside the house at about four o'clock in the morning. No one ever actually saw this woman, she was only ever heard.

Being single and free at the time, Tony decided to 'up sticks' and rent a flat on Wellesley Road, and he sat up all night with a reel-to-reel tape recorder at the ready. After only four days of waiting, he heard the phantom crier. The time, he noted, was five minutes to four, and he even managed to record the eerie voice. The voice seemed to pass down the street and then gradually fade away. Tony thought he could also hear footsteps. On the following morning, an ambulance pulled up at a house a few doors away. An old woman had fallen downstairs and died in the night. The neighbours said they thought they had heard a loud noise in the old woman's house at four o'clock in the morning.

Tony waited for weeks after that hair-raising night, but the Crying Woman of the Dingle seemed to have retired, at least for the time being. He racked his brains, trying to work out what the nature of this ghost was and why she was haunting one specific area of Liverpool. He was completely stumped, and the reports of the crying woman gradually died out.

But a year later, Tony was dating a woman named Betty, who lived in Falkner Square. Betty's previous boyfriend had been a detective with Merseyside Police. This detective had told her that the stories of the Crying Woman of the Dingle were true, which had surprised her. The detective said that the Crying Woman was the ghost of a prostitute who had been murdered in the Dingle a few years back. The girl had been brutally bludgeoned to death by a client at four in the morning, and had walked the streets crying for help, but no one would open their doors to the poor woman. Police had followed the trail of blood and had found her battered body huddled in an alleyway. The girl was from a well-to-do family, and had naively fallen into prostitution in an attempt to survive on the streets when she had run away from home.

When Tony researched Betty's story and found it to be true, he searched for the specific alley she had been found in, and left a wreath at the spot where she had been murdered, and painted a small cross on the wall.

Dead Man's Hand

This is a very strange story (even as my stories go). In May 1980, a woman in the Old Swan area of Liverpool, Mrs Hollingdon, was putting on make-up as she looked in a mirror. As she was applying foundation, she noticed a slight swelling under her chin – a lump! Mrs Hollingdon panicked. It did not feel painful, but she feared the worst. She rushed off to see her doctor, who examined it and then referred her to a specialist at the Royal Hospital.

The news was not good, the specialist told Mrs Hollingdon that the swelling – or goitre, to use the proper term – was malignant. He considered that operating on the lump would be too dangerous, as it was within a fraction of an inch of a jugular vein, nor did he think that hacking out chunks from the floor of Mrs Hollingdon's mouth would be conducive to any possible recovery. However, the specialist did suggest a course of radiotherapy.

Mrs Hollingdon and her husband both wept when they were given the bad news, but Mr Hollingdon had an idea in the back of his mind, a very slim idea. He was originally from the Lake District, and had known a woman in a village up there who had cured his mother once when she had found a lump in her breast. That woman would have to be in her eighties by now, if indeed she was still alive. The old woman, Mrs Bell, had been regarded as something of a witch because of the way she used very unorthodox methods to bring about a cure. She was known to use herbs and all sorts of concoctions and remedies.

Mr Hollingdon convinced his wife to take a trip up the M6 to see if they could find old Mrs Bell. The couple drove into the little village which lay at the foot of the Cumbrian Mountains. The place had hardly changed since he last saw it. The Hollingdons had to park up their car because the narrow cobbled roads were impassable in the area where Mary Bell had lived. Mr Hollingdon called into a tiny Post Office to enquire about Mrs Bell's whereabouts – and, by a strange coincidence, bumped into the very woman he was looking for. She looked remarkably youthful and sprightly for her age. The old woman invited Mr Hollingdon and his wife to her home, where she took a look at the swelling on the Liverpool woman's neck and her brows immediately furrowed. She said she was sorry but she had no medicine or herbs of any kind to treat the condition, but instead suggested something which made the couple's blood run cold.

"If you could stroke that lump with the hand of a freshly deceased man, it would surely go," she said, obviously aware of the impact of her suggestion. She then gave a garbled account of the black magic behind her suggestion, but the Hollingdons were too stunned and disappointed to take it in. They left soon after and Mr Hollingdon decided that it would be best to go home straightaway to Merseyside.

But Mrs Hollingdon did not want to return home. She wanted to rest for a few days in a hotel. So, Mr Hollingdon, anxious to do whatever his distraught and weary wife wanted, drove to an hotel not too far from Kendal. He booked a double room, and all that night he hugged his wife in bed and tried to reassure her that everything would be fine.

"Wonder if it would have worked – the dead man's hand thing?" Mrs Hollingdon mused.

"Old Mrs Bell's probably gone senile, but she used to be nothing short of a miracle worker. She cured my mother."

"Ah well," sighed Mrs Hollingdon, in a defeatist tone. "It looks like radiotherapy, I haven't got much choice."

Her husband clutched her close, and in the most cheerful voice he could muster, joked: "Unless we can go to a mortuary and find a dead man."

Mrs Hollingdon gently smiled, able to see the funny side of the old woman's preposterous suggestion.

Just as they were about to settle down for a good night's sleep, the couple heard a voice cry out, just once, next door. After a few moment's silence, they heard a woman exclaim, "Oh my God!"

Mr Hollingdon shot out of bed. He opened the door and peeped down the deserted, dimly-lit hotel corridor. A maid came out of the room next door looking very anxious, and she ran off down the corridor. Mr Hollingdon crept down the passage and peeped in the room next door. An elderly man was hanging out of the bed at an awkward angle with his eyes wide open. The upper set of his false teeth were on the floor. He looked dead. Perhaps he had suffered a fatal heart attack or stroke.

As Mr Hollingdon stood looking at the poor man, Mrs Bell's bizarre recommendation came into his head. He raced back to his hotel room, and pulled his wife out of bed. She sleepily followed, assuming there must be a fire by the way he was hurrying her along. He pushed her into the next room and told her to sit down next to the old man who had just expired. Mrs Hollingdon recoiled in horror when she saw the body, but her husband pushed her to the floor. He then took hold of the dead man's clammy hand, already going cold, and he pressed it against his wife's throat and stroked it several times. As his wife struggled to suppress her revulsion, he prayed out loud: "Oh! Please God, make this work."

Voices and footsteps could be heard outside the room. The maid was bringing the hotel manager and a doctor up the stairs and showing them to the correct room. The couple rushed back to their own room, trembling. Mrs Hollingdon was sobbing.

Incredibly, within a week, the goitre on Mrs Hollingdon's neck was gone. It is true that some tumours can, very rarely, shrink and vanish. Cancer can certainly go into remission at any time, but a specialist who examined Mrs Hollingdon could not explain how her lump had completely vanished within the space of a week.

Murder Foreseen

In May 1950, a 32-year-old Tuebrook woman, Mary Jones, started work at the Littlewoods Pool's firm on Edge Lane, near the Botanic Park.

Mary was separated from her husband, and considered herself to be single. Her five-year-old son Bobby was staying with her grandmother for the time being. One night she went out to a pub with a few friends, and she met a very handsome man of about forty. He was rather shabbily dressed, but Mary had never seen anyone so attractive. He had curly black hair and unusual, sky-blue eyes. He was also quite stocky. He smiled a few times at Mary, then came over and asked her if he could buy her a drink. Mary accepted, and as the night wore on, he and she left the others and went to have a drink in a corner of the pub.

The man's name was Ted Lawless and, at first, he was very reluctant to say just exactly what he did for a living but then he changed his mind and decided to tell Mary. He was a scrap metal merchant. Mary did not really care what Ted did, because already she thought there was something very charismatic about him.

Ted lived near Fontenoy Gardens, where he owned and ran a small scrapyard, but he happened to be in Tuebrook on this particular night, to buy some old lead pipes from the pub landlord.

When the pub closed, Ted kissed Mary and arranged to see her again at the Locarno. She was very excited about the date and when it finally came, they danced the night away. Mary still had not told Ted that she had a husband, and this kept nagging at her, she should have told him when they first met. When they left the Locarno, Ted convinced Mary to go home with him and she stayed the night. The following morning, he could not hide his feelings and asked her to live with him, but she made excuses, saying she had to look after her mother, who was not too well at the moment.

Ted Lawless held Mary's face close to his: "I'm of Romany descent. My grandmother was part gypsy, and I can just look into your eyes and know you're not telling me the truth," he said.

"What are you talking about?" asked Mary, averting her eyes and feeling distinctly uncomfortable.

Ted grabbed her hand and examined her palm, he frowned and announced that she was married and had a son. Mary thought he must have learnt this information from one of her friends.

"Who told you, huh? Was it Maureen?" she demanded, presuming it was her friend at Littlewoods who had told him.

Ted explained that he could read this information from Mary herself. He reached out and hugged her, declaring passionately, "It doesn't matter Mary, I can't let you go."

A week later, something unusual happened. Mary visited the scrapyard near Fontenoy Gardens and found it deserted. The gates were chained up. A man across the street told Mary that Mr Lawless had moved away and that the yard had closed down. Someone said Lawless had moved to Preston.

Mary was frantic, and heartbroken – just when she thought she had found happiness. A few days later, a letter arrived at Littlewoods Pools, addressed to Mary Jones. The letter was from Ted and in it, he explained that he had been forced to leave Mary after a experiencing three terrifying nightmares. He had dreamt that he had strangled her after he had found her in the embrace of a man. In the dream he had knifed the man, and then strangled her in a fit of jealous rage. The same realistic dream had recurred on the following night. Ted explained that he had had such dreams before, and they had always come true, so he regarded them as forebodings, not to be ignored. In the third dream, he had been reading a copy of the *Liverpool Echo*, and the double murder he had committed had made front page news. The dream had been so real, Lawless was even able to read the print in the article, and he saw that the name of the man he had knifed had been Patrick Berry, aged 33, from Fairfield. Finally, Lawless had seen a noose dangle down before his eyes, and he had woken up in a cold sweat.

Mary assumed that Ted had made up this strange story as an excuse to leave her, as she knew no one named Patrick Berry. But five months later, a new barman started work at the pub which Mary frequented with her friends. The man's name was Pat, and it transpired that he was from Fairfield. After a short while he started to court Mary Jones. Naturally, Mary soon wanted to know her new boyfriend's full name and she recoiled in shock when she learnt that his surname was Berry. Without explaining her motives, she immediately stopped seeing him there and then.

But for the Grace of God

There's an old saying: 'There, but for the grace of God go I,' which means do not condemn anyone who has taken a wrong turning in life, because it could happen to any of us. This proverb certainly applies to the following strange story, which was told to me recently by a very rich and successful Knowsley businessman.

One evening in July 1999, Derek, a 45-year-old businessman from Knowsley, was in Bold Street with a friend from work called Tony. As the two were passing a shop doorway, a beggar held out a grimey hand and asked: "Could you spare any change please lads?"

Without giving him a second glance, Derek said something which ended with the word 'off' and walked on. Tony, however, stopped and gave the man some money.

"You shouldn't encourage them, mate," said Derek, looking at the hunched figure with pure contempt.

"Remember that old saying, Derek, 'There but for the grace of God go I.'" And then, turning to the beggar, Tony said, "just ignore him. Go and get yourself some hot food."

Derek shook his head in disbelief and the two of them walked on to a club.

On the following day, in Knowsley, a *Big Issue* seller asked Derek and Tony if they would like to buy a copy. Tony said he already had that week's copy and walked on, but Derek reached into his inside pocket. The vendor thought Derek was getting out his wallet and started to fold up the *Big Issue* for him. But instead, Derek got out a small, folded up document and with a sneer, he handed it to the homeless man.

"Here, this is called a housing benefit form; you fill it in and you won't be homeless anymore."

"Derek, for God's sake, stop messing about, come on," Tony sighed.

The *Big Issue* seller muttered, "Have a nice day sir," and despondently unfolded the top copy of his pile of magazines.

Derek smirked, thinking he had made a really clever joke. However, that night, at ten minutes to eleven, something happened which chilled his blood. He had phoned for a taxi and was leaving a pub called the Derby Arms on Knowsley Lane. He walked out of the pub to get some fresh air, and saw the same beggar whom he had insulted in Bold Street a few days previously. The man was standing in the shadows outside the pub, but Derek was able to recognise him immediately. The taxi turned up that second, and Derek hurried into it.

"That beggar's weird isn't he?" he said to the cabby, clicking his seat belt on.

"Where? Which beggar?" said the cabby, checking his mirrors and looking around. He could see no one.

Derek was startled to notice that the beggar was no longer lurking in the shadows, and yet there was no one in sight, either way, on the stretch of road.

On the following day, at 5pm, Derek was in Liverpool city centre, shopping with his girlfriend, Jenni, at Wade Smith and a few other stores. The couple had parked their car at the bottom of Brownlow Hill, and as they were heading back to the car park, Derek suddenly made an unplanned detour, following a long-winded route up Bold Street. When Jenni asked him why he was going that way, Derek said that he wanted to see if the beggar he had seen up in Knowsley was sitting in his usual doorway, because he wanted to ask him what he had been doing up near the Derby Arms.

"Oh let it go, Derek," said Jenni, pulling on his arm. "My feet are killing me and I'm dying for a cup of tea."

But Derek was determined to find the beggar. However, when he got to that doorway on Bold Street, Derek saw something which sent an unpleasant shiver down his spine. The grubby-looking man slumped dejectedly in the doorway, with his stubbled face and greasy hair, was an exact double of himself.

Jenni was speechless, and Derek just stood there, gaping at the unfortunate man. He felt his heart palpitating. Derek had a small but distinctive mole on his left cheek, and so did the beggar in the doorway. It was not as if this man was a twin, or a look-alike – he was Derek himself, sitting there. The strange thing was, that the doppelganger never once looked at Derek, but kept looking down at the pavement with a slight grin playing on his face.

Derek and Jenni hurried away from Bold Street without saying a word, but when they reached the car park, and were safely back inside their car, they sat for ages going over what they had just witnessed. This inexplicable event took place in 1999, and Derek and Jenni still refuse to venture anywhere near Bold Street.

Spectral City

There have been many reports of phantom villages and towns over the years. Just after dawn one day in 1951, some Israeli soldiers, British officers and a group of Arabs, all witnessed the appearance of some orange groves, a flowing river, and a huge palace surrounded by streets in Palestine. Minutes later, the strange city was slowly replaced by the familiar stretch of barren, rocky desert. Such phantom villages and cities have also been seen in Britain. In the Lake District, a quaint looking town is said to appear out of the mists, like Brigadoon, but people are warned never to approach such phantasmagorical towns, because tradition has it that they are gateways to Hell.

This is a very intriguing story from the 1970s. In 1975, an Ormskirk man, Mike Burgess, and his cousin, Alan Brown, from Chester, decided to spend a few weeks at a caravan site on the Isle of Anglesey. Both men were aged forty at the time. They parked their caravan at a point overlooking Holyhead Bay. Halfway through the holiday, Alan and Mike met two women and went to a local pub with them. Later that night they left the pub, and Alan and his girl went their separate ways, after arranging to meet again the following night. Mike Burgess invited the girl he had met back to their caravan.

As Mike and the young woman were walking back to the caravan with Alan, she suddenly pointed to a hillside and shouted, "Look!" They all looked in the direction she was pointing and saw a collection of very old looking buildings in the distance on the hillside. They seemed to be Tudor-styled houses with the characteristic black and white magpie stripes. Alan Brown was intrigued, as he had not noticed the village before. He was certain that there had only been vast fields at that spot just hours earlier. He impulsively decided to go and investigate, even though the Welsh girl tried to talk him out of it. Alan took no notice. His last words were: "I'm going to have a look."

Mike and the girl walked on and went into the caravan. They peered out through the windows in the direction of the hillside. There was absolutely no sign of the village. Convinced that something very strange was taking place, the couple left the caravan and walked about a quarter of a mile towards the spot. They came upon a field with a large purple patch of heather growing in it. There was no sign of Alan, so they started shouting out for him, but got no reply. After searching all night, they were so worried that they alerted police, who subsequently put Alan

Brown on the missing persons' register. No one came forward with any information and he failed to get in touch with his family. Apparently he has never been found to this day.

*

Strangely enough, in 1905, just a few miles from the scene of the phantom village, near a place called Elim, a spectral city was once reported by several people, including a 15-year-old girl and her little sister who were picnicking in the area. Their descriptions of a 'golden shimmering city', that briefly appeared on a hill, were predictably dismissed as religious mania, as a Methodist revival had recently taken place in that part of Wales. Whether the two incidents were connected has not been established and nor can we know with any certainty whether the visions were a mirage from the ancient past, or even the distant future.

Sinister School Inspectors

Clutching both his parents' hands, a small boy walked into the consulting room of Dr J Ford Thomson, a psychiatrist at the Education Office at Wolverhampton, in the winter of 1956. The seven-year-old was causing great anxiety to his parents and teachers, not because he was struggling with his schoolwork, or behaving badly in any way, but because he appeared to be a genius.

This small boy apparently knew the right answers to the most complicated problems of astronomy, physics and mathematics. His IQ was 140, but what amazed the psychiatrist most was his apparent ability to move objects with his mind. This was not an isolated case, according to the British Medical Research Council, because they secretly tested 5,000 schoolchildren all over England – including Liverpool – over an 18 month period. The conclusion to this secret study was that there had been 'a sudden rise in the level of intelligence', perhaps caused by barely detectable amounts of Strontium 90, a radioactive substance that drifted all over the world after the atomic bombs were dropped on Japan. It was hypothesised that his Strontium 90 had mutated the genes and somehow improved them. In other words, the Government discovered that a new race of young people was appearing, endowed with superior intellectual powers.

A second secret screening programme was carried out in Britain, France, Australia and America between 1976 and 1977. Specially appointed inspectors were sent to various schools to test the pupils, and what they allegedly uncovered was amazing. Around this time, there was a documentary on BBC2 called *Open Door*, and it reported on this secret Government programme. A teacher claimed that inspectors at a Liverpool school discovered three telepathic children who were able to read each other's minds. They were tested with special cards called Zener Cards, which have symbols like stars and wavy lines and such like on them, and the children correctly named every card the inspector looked at. Children in other schools, could detect and describe hidden objects by sweeping their hands over sealed boxes.

I wonder if any readers out there who went to school in the 1970s, remember being tested by these mysterious inspectors ...

Just a Game

I often received letters from people asking if it is safe to dabble with the ouija board. The answer I always give is: no, the ouija board is not a toy, even though toymakers Fisher Price and Waddingtons license so-called ouija board 'games'. The following true story is a case in point. It comes from an old magazine called *Destiny*, now out of print.

In the 1970s, Liverpool DJ, Kenny Everett, in a serious mood for once, related the following story:

'After supper one night, two friends came over to our home and we decided to try and hold a séance by using a ouija board. We all sat around the table, nice and cosy, playing with the glass and asking the spirit of the board different questions – when a message came through for my friend John.

The spirit said that it was a message from a girl, then spelt out her name. John immediately said that he knew a girl with that name. In fact, he had been engaged to her and had only just broken off the engagement. But, she was alive and well, he asserted, so the message could not possibly be from her.

We then asked the spirit girl when she had died and were staggered when the glass spelled out the answer: 'NOON TODAY'. As we asked more questions we discovered that the girl had gassed herself after having a row with her mother. She said that she still loved John and regretted breaking up. Asked where she was now, she gave us the address of a mortuary miles away! John had gone very pale and said that if this was a joke, it had gone too far and was in very bad taste.

The amazing thing was that none us there, apart from John, even knew the girl's name, let alone that she had been engaged to him. We were all very badly shaken, and to put his mind at rest, we told him to telephone the mortuary.

While we all stood by, holding our breath. He telephoned the mortuary and learned that every detail the glass had told us about the girl was true. John was visibly shaking by now, not only because of the terrible news, but because of something else which the spirit girl had communicated through the glass. Her final words had been: "Join me".'

Kenny Everett's wife said she had never seen her husband be so serious as he was in the days following the ouija board incident. Fortunately Kenny and his friends realised that they were dabbling in things they did not understand and could not control, and they never messed with the ouija board again.

Terror on the M62

The following mysterious incident was related to me in September 2001, by a well-known Liverpool comedian whom I cannot identify. He stipulated that he would only relate the full facts of the bizarre and scary tale if I would give him my word that I would never identify him. I shall therefore have to call the comedian 'Bob'.

In the early 1990s, Bob drove up the M62 to Manchester, where he was due to perform a comedy routine as part of a cabaret show. As usual, Bob's performance was very warmly received by the audience, and, in appreciation, he decided to go back onstage for a further twenty minutes. While he was performing his additional material, he noticed a beautiful-looking woman of about 25 or 30 years of age, sitting at a table. She was smiling at Bob, and she reminded him of the Seventies film actress, Farrah Fawcett Majors. After he had finished his comedy act and had basked in the audience's enthusiastic applause, Bob went backstage and changed, then the manager of the club escorted him to a specially-reserved table for a meal and a drink.

Just before the next performer took to the stage, Bob made his way over to the table where the woman was sitting alone, and asked her if she would care to join him. The woman smiled, and accepted without any hesitation. She was very tall and looked even more attractive at closer quarters. She had sapphire-blue eyes, and long blonde hair. In a soft voice, she said, "My name's Danielle." Her accent was not a local one, but was difficult to place.

Bob ordered champagne and was soon flirting with Danielle. The woman, however, refused the champagne and preferred to sip mineral water. There was a 'stay-behind' at the club, and it was not long before Bob and Danielle were dancing slowly, tightly embracing each other. He learned that the reason Danielle was on her own was that her boyfriend had arranged to meet her at the club, but had not turned up for some reason. She told him that she lived in St Helens, and Bob said that, as she had not been drinking, she could drive him home to Merseyside in his car. Danielle was not keen and instead preferred that Bob stay overnight at her home until he was fit enough to drive in the morning. At 3am, Bob and Danielle left the club in Manchester and walked through the chilly night air towards the club car park. Danielle shivered in her sleeveless top, so Bob gave her his leather jacket. Danielle had to strap Bob's seatbelt on for him because he was so intoxicated. Minutes later, the couple embarked on the return journey down the M62. During the journey, Bob fumbled for the controls of the car radio, but Danielle's hand intercepted his, and so, the couple sat in silence as the car sped along the motorway.

Suddenly stirring from his alcohol-induced doze, Bob turned to look at Danielle and saw something that still gives him nightmares to this day. The girl's beautiful features had contorted into what can only be described as a demonic scowl. Her head swivelled towards him and her eyes turned blood red, and her mouth opened wide – twice as wide as a normal mouth – to reveal a fearsome array of pointed teeth.

The comedian instantly became sober, but felt faint and breathless with the shock. The girl sitting in the driving seat of his car must be some sort of supernatural entity and was driving him goodness knows where. As if it was able to read his mind, the thing in the driving seat screamed with manic laughter and suicidally zig-zagged between the lanes of the motorway. Bob was not a religious man, but he suddenly found himself imploring, "Jesus, please save me".

The car screeched into a 180-degree turn and slid off the hard shoulder onto a slip road, then veered into a ditch. Bob opened the door and tried to get out, but in his blind panic, he forgot to unclick his seatbelt. He cried out desperately for help and looked back in terror at the seat beside him; it was empty, except for his leather jacket. There was no trace of the fiend who had been masquerading as a woman.

The police found Bob wandering along the hard shoulder of the M62, and he gabbled out his bizarre tale, but was not believed. The police checked the club, and the management confirmed that Bob had left with a woman and that she had driven him home. Not one person at the club had any idea who 'Danielle' was. Bob was badly shaken by the spine-chilling incident, and has never appeared at the Manchester club since.

Freudian Timeslip

In the year 1892, a beautiful woman of about 50 years of age was admitted to the private, richly-furnished consulting room of Sigmund Freud in Vienna. An enormous collection of Egyptian and Greek antiquities and leather-bound volumes lined the walls of the room from floor to ceiling. His client was a rich British widow from Liverpool called Isobelle McAllister. Contrary to his popular image as a cerebral cold fish, Freud could be something of a ladies' man, and he was immediately captivated by Mrs McAllister, who obviously belonged to high society. She was wearing an exotic Indian headscarf, strings of pearls, and a sleeveless royal blue silk gown which was very risqué in those times. The psychoanalyst greeted Isobelle by kissing her knuckle, then invited her to lie on a comfortable, padded, rug-covered couch. Freud sat out of sight in a leather-backed armchair at right angles to the couch, and lit up a Don Pedro cigar – the twelfth he had smoked that day.

"Relax first, and when you are ready, talk," intoned Freud.

Mrs McAllister relaxed, closed her eyes, then began: "For many years, since I was a child, I have been haunted by a dream."

"Tell me about this dream," Freud's voice drifted out of the ectoplasmic blue cloud of his cigar smoke.

"I see the Crucifixion in this dream. It doesn't seem to be a dream though, because it is so real, so vivid, and I know what is going to happen, because I have lived through this dream so many times before, over and over."

"Who was being crucified?"

"Jesus of Nazareth. I see him and the two thieves on crosses and the crowd are like monsters, jeering and laughing."

Freud had just learned several very effective hypnotic techniques from the great hypnotist, Charcot, and he decided to hypnotise Mrs Isobelle McAllister, in order to delve into her subconscious. She fell into a light trance, and Freud told her that the persistent dream would begin soon. Freud was then quite surprised, because when he asked if she could describe the dream, she started to talk in an unknown language. A university colleague was invited in, and when he heard Isobelle, he immediately recognised the language she was speaking. It was Aramaic, the language Jesus had spoken. Freud's associate wrote down several pages of the Aramaic spoken by the Englishwoman, and then had it all translated. Freud then used his hypnotic suggestion and instructed his patient to talk in English. For almost an hour, Mrs McAllister gave a disturbing eyewitness account of the crucifixion of a man she called Yeshua, a controversial and outspoken man, whom she described as a teacher and miracle worker. She also described him as being of above average height, and wearing a long pigtail. His eyes had some strange quality about them and few could stare at them for long. She said the man's mother and a number of other women were watching the crucifixion, and his mother was almost fainting, but was being supported by two friends. Jesus was on a T-shaped cross, and the Roman guards were hitting and prodding the men on the other crosses with lances and a ladder.

Mrs McAllister also mentioned a curious detail that was later backed up by historians. She said the nails were not driven into Jesus's hands, but through the small bones of his wrists. She also described how the Romans talked about a titulus – a small plaque which they fixed on a stick and nailed above Jesus's head. On this plaque they wrote mocking graffiti in Latin.

Freud asked Mrs McAllister to describe her regressive background, and discovered she had been a prostitute who had received forgiveness from Jesus. Her brother had been the enigmatic man in the Garden of Gethsemane who was grabbed by the Romans but fled naked, leaving the guard clutching the sheet he had been wearing.

Freud was very disturbed by what seemed like a case of reincarnation, and it was a turning point for the psychoanalyst. He avoided mentioning the case in public though, not just because of the Jewish view of Jesus being a prophet; Freud also did not want to jeopardise his lucrative career by associating himself with the widely-dismissed world of the supernatural. However, just before he died, in 1939, he declared that if he had his life to live again, he would dedicate himself to studying the paranormal.

Reunited by a Ghost

In 1974, a Bebington baker, Frank Medley, started to seriously date a Liverpool girl, Jane Gerard. They were both aged twenty. Frank used to travel across the River Mersey to Liverpool most nights between his shifts at the bakery and visit Jane at her home near Sefton Park. In the summer, he would walk her back home through Sefton Park, and they would often stop by an old weeping willow, where he would embrace and kiss her for a while.

The couple eventually married, and were quite happy at first, but somehow they let the love they had for one another slip away, and soon, Frank was having an affair. Jane found out and in turn embarked on an affair to get back at her unfaithful husband. Things spiralled out of control from there, and in 1982, the couple were divorced.

The mutual hatred that divorce often causes was certainly present between Jane and Frank. Often they would pass on the street without acknowledging one another, refusing to even nod. Oddly enough, they both ended up living in the same street overlooking Sefton Park, and they both remained single.

One hot summer evening, Frank was on the veranda of his flat, when he saw something very strange. By the faint light of a crescent moon, he detected two familiar figures strolling across the park towards the old weeping willow tree. Frank ran to get his binoculars, but when he looked through them, he found that the tree was in the way. The silhouettes he had seen had looked exactly like himself and Jane when they were first dating. It was just like looking back in time.

Frank quickly put on his shoes and dashed downstairs. He crossed the road and walked parallel to the railings, trying to watch the couple in the park out the corner of his eye.

His heart skipped a beat when he realised that the young couple were wearing 1970s-type clothes; even down to her flares. Then a familiar voice behind Frank called out his name. Frank spun around, startled. It was Jane, his ex-wife. She was also looking at the couple in the park. She too had noticed them while walking her dog.

"Isn't that weird?" she said.

"Oh. Er, hi! I'm glad you're here seeing this. I thought I was going nuts."

They went into the park together with the dog, and when they reached the weeping willow tree, they discovered that there was no one there.

"That smell!" said Frank, sniffing the air.

"Smells like Charlie," Jane said. "I haven't smelt that smell for years."

The atmosphere was very calm and still by the willow tree. 'Charlie' was the name of the perfume she used to wear a lot in the Seventies and the area round the tree seemed to be impregnated with it.

The couple lingered round the spot, probably thinking about the days when they had been young and their love fresh. Frank grabbed Jane's hand as she started to walk back towards the park gates, and expected her to pull it away, but she just looked at him.

"There's nothing on TV tonight, why are you in such a hurry to get back?" he said.

Jane laughed and looked up at the night sky, "Look at those stars," she smiled, "We're just a moment compared to them."

Frank and Jane started seeing one another again and later re-married, and those mysterious shades of yesterday, those figures in the park, whatever or whoever they were, were their inspiration.

Golden Opportunity

During the course of my research into Liverpool's past, I came across a real gem: a funny little story about a schoolboy who told a white lie, just to seem like a hero.

In December 1959, twelve-year-old Douggie was mooching through his parents' bedroom at his home in Gerrard Gardens. He was looking for his Christmas presents, and he found them hidden on top of an old wardrobe. His heart skipped a beat when he saw a banjo-shaped parcel, wrapped in brown paper. Douggie only wanted one of two things for Christmas – a banjo or a racing bike.

Sadly, his heart sank when he felt the parcelled-up 'banjo' and realised that it was in fact a badly-wrapped bat and ball set. The child sulked and walked downtown to ogle at the bikes in the shop windows. He stopped at a shop called Cundles in Whitechapel and pressed his nose up against the window to scrutinise a silver, chrome-finished, racing bike with five gears. It was love at first sight. Unfortunately, the bike was seven pounds. Douggie knew his mother would never be able to afford such an expensive Christmas present. The child muttered a fervent little prayer to himself, asking for the seven pounds. He promised that he would be as good as gold if he could just have that bike.

It was starting to get dark, so Douggie set off for home through Queen's Square. He came across a huge woman wearing a luxurious fur coat arguing with a man. The woman was Rosie Fagan, wife of Liverpool millionaire, Frank Fagan, who owned a string of fruit warehouses in the North West. Rosie had just had a heated argument with Frank over something, and insisted that he drive her home. He told her to get lost, and continued chatting with the costermongers of Queens Square, many of whom were employed by him. Rosie Fagan stormed off across the square after demanding the keys to a truck so she could drive herself home. Young Douggie loved watching a dramatic row, and he followed Mrs Fagan across Queen's Square. Rosie clambered into the truck, and shortly afterwards let out a scream which made Douggie jump. She almost fell out of the truck screaming that there was a big poisonous snake in the vehicle on the seat.

A bespectacled passerby prodded the snake with a stick then announced: "It's a conga eel, they're deadly! Get the police!" and he backed off.

Douggie inched forward, intrigued, but the man with the specs shouted: "Get back, son, it's a killer!"

Rosie's legs almost buckled under her, and a man selling copies of the *Liverpool Echo* steadied her.

"What's a snake doing in there?" she panted.

"It'll have come off the stuff at the docks, love," said the *Echo* seller knowledgeably. "Our kid found a tarantula in a crate of plums once." He pointed to his cigarette, "Honest girl, may this thing choke me. A tarantula big as me hand."

Douggie peered into the cab and saw the snake. He beamed a smile, then looked around to make sure that everyone was watching. He ran up to the truck and climbed into the vehicle before anyone could stop him. Immediately there were screams and gasps of horror. Douggie wrestled with the snake, then jumped out of the cab, holding its curled up body. He shook it and ran towards a grid, hysterical people diving out of his way. The boy bravely stuffed the snake down a grid, then backed away, wiping his hands on his trousers. Three men closed in on the boy. A taxi driver asked: "You alright, lad?" While another onlooker scolded him: "You idiot, that was a stupid thing to do."

Douggie smiled and simply said: "It bit me, but it never broke the skin."

A crowd gathered at the grid and the braver ones peered down into it, but it was too dark to see anything. Rosie Fagan made an enormous fuss of the boy, then opened her huge packed purse and handed him five pounds. Douggie thanked her, hardly able to believe his luck and, after basking in all the attention, immediately knew what he would do. He set off for Cundles and started haggling with the shopkeeper for the bike. Just then, the shopkeeper's brother, who had witnessed the boy's heroic deed, walked in and told his brother all about it. The shopkeeper was so impressed that he gave him the bike for nothing.

Then the truth of what had really happened leaked out. The driver of the truck where the snake had been spotted wondered where his leopardskin steering wheel cover had gone. The bare iron steering wheel was freezing in December, so he had bought a leopardskin steering wheel cover to put on it; this cover, with its leopardskin spots, had been mistaken for a snake. Crafty Douggie had recognised the so-called snake for what it really was, and had seen his golden opportunity. Luckily for Douggie, he was never traced, and Rosie Fagan saw the funny side anyway, but it was a good Christmas that year for a poor schoolboy in Gerrard Gardens.

The Highest Judge

This is an amazing story, well documented in the United States. In December 1893 at Columbia, Mississippi, 200 people threw their hats into the air and cheered. Festivities commenced and the saloons handed out drinks on the house. The unlikely cause of the celebrations and high jinks, was the lynching of a young black man, who had allegedly raped a farmer's 15-year-old daughter. The sheriff more or less turned a blind eye to the lynching, and he himself was suspected of being a member of the local branch of the Ku Klux Klan, who had been responsible for it.

However, a fortnight later, in an almost copycat incident, another woman was raped at knifepoint by a masked man in front of her children. The traumatised victim told the sheriff's men that the attacker was definitely white, because she had glimpsed his bare hands and parts of his face. Nevertheless, another black youth was targeted by the racist mob, but luckily he caught wind of what was going on and escaped by fleeing the town. The frustrated lynch mob, seeking vengeance, burned down his family's home.

Around this time, a preacher called Joseph Levine, came to town and was appalled and sickened by the bigotry, lynchings and kangaroo courts. He had emigrated to America from Sefton, Lancashire, three years before, after allegedly experiencing a religious vision. Levine burst into a saloon in Columbia on one occasion, leapt up onto a table, and spontaneously delivered a sermon. He declared that God was the highest judge of all, and that the state of a man's soul was the only thing that mattered – the colour of his skin was of absolutely no importance. He was heckled and booed but persevered with his message. Then one rowdy citizen fetched a bullwhip and tried to strike the preacher, but as he drew back the whip, it lashed out the eye of his own son. This enraged the crowd even more and Levine was attacked and was lucky to escape with his life. A local widow gave him refuge, but said he would have to leave in a few days, otherwise the mob would destroy her home for sheltering a man who sympathised with the black folk.

On 7 February of that year, a young white man named Will Purvis was taken to the town's gallows to be hanged for the murder of a farmer in Columbia. However, it was widely rumoured in the town that a man named Joe Beard had actually killed the farmer, so the preacher suicidally intervened. The 3,000-strong crowd spat at him and threw stones at him as he managed to climb onto the stage supporting the gallows. The hangman had already placed the noose around Will Purvis's neck and tied his hands behind his back. The sheriff, Irvin Magee, and his deputy, grabbed the preacher and held him firmly. They turned Levine towards Purvis.

"You can watch him die, preacherman," sneered the deputy.

Joseph Levine suddenly cried out: "I call upon the Highest Judge of all to halt this injustice. I call upon the Lord my God!"

The trapdoor snapped open, and Will Purvis was plunging to his doom – when suddenly, the noose became unknotted and slipped over the condemned man's head. Purvis landed on his feet below the stage, then slumped in a state of shock. The hangman examined the dangling rope. He was completely mystified. The people in the crowd gasped as one, then watched, silent and tense, seeming to regard the freak incident as a miracle. The sheriff nervously announced that the rope had been made of grass which had been too wiry to keep a knot. Will Purvis was led back onto the stage and a new noose was made and checked and placed over his head. Something strange then took place that has never been explained to this day. The people in the front rows started to gabble in an unknown language. It sounded like complete gibberish. Many thought they had started to speak in tongues, which is a well reported phenomenon during outbreaks of religious mania. The crowd surged towards the stage and demanded that the sheriff reprieve Purvis. The sheriff refused at first but became intimidated by the angry, babbling crowd, and had to bend to their wishes.

Purvis was re-tried and found guilty, but friends and supporters attacked the prison and freed him. Purvis, still professing his innocence, later surrendered and his death sentence was commuted to life imprisonment. The jurors who had found him guilty had been twelve notorious members of the lynching party. At the trial, the distraught Purvis had ominously warned the jurors that he would live to see the last one of them die.

Several years later, the real killer, Joe Beard, confessed on his deathbed to the murder of the Columbia farmer, and Will Purvis was exonerated and freed from gaol. Oddly, every one of the jurors who had wrongly sentenced him died, straight after one another, so Purvis did indeed outlive them as he had predicted he would. The rope that miraculously unknotted itself has since been analysed many times, and no defect could be found. To his dying day, Will Purvis believed that God had intervened to save him.

Gridlock

Many foolish things have been done in the attempt to win the heart of a woman, and the following is an extreme example.

In 1811, in the luxurious setting of the new Exchange Coffee Rooms in Liverpool, two businessmen, both aged 55, were having a discussion about who they thought was the most beautiful woman in the city. Daniel Doyle insisted that a young lady named Henrietta Shelbourne was the finest creature he had ever set eyes upon, and his friend Nathan Kingsley said that he had to agree. Mr Doyle commented that he and his bachelor friend had to resign themselves to the fact that they were far too old for Miss Shelbourne, who had just turned 21, but Mr Kingsley disagreed.

Mr Doyle sighed, then sank into deep thought as he puffed on his pipe. After some time spent in wistful contemplation, he announced: "I have heard that Henrietta will be attending a ball at Colonel Denney's house in Belgravia on Sunday."

"Really?" replied Kingsley with a dreamy smile.

The two men decided to attend the ball, just to be in the presence of the delightful Miss Shelbourne, so they boarded the train for London. During the journey, Daniel Doyle had too much whiskey to drink, and he bet his friend a thousand guineas that he could win Miss Shelbourne's heart. Mr Kingsley readily accepted the wager.

Doyle and Kingsley attended the ball, and when they saw Henrietta Shelbourne, they both felt instantly rejuvenated. She looked amazingly beautiful in a sparkling, sequinned, sky-blue dress, and she was surrounded by a flock of admirers as usual. She was something of a wit – always laughing – and this was part of the charisma that attracted men to her, like a moth to a flame.

As the night wore on, Daniel Doyle saw his opportunity and he engineered the chance to dance with Henrietta. He was thoroughly intoxicated, both with whiskey and with love, and he passionately beseeched the lady of his dreams: "What has a man to do to win your heart?"

Henrietta threw back her head, smiling broadly, then said, "He must make me feel like the most special thing in the world". Then she giggled coquettishly, and pressed her nose against Daniel Doyle's nose. "Bring London to a standstill for me," she added, intimately. Her face was pressed so close, that Mr Doyle felt her fluttering eyelashes against his cheek. It felt as if as if an electric shock had coursed through his body. Her rose-perfumed scent filled his head, intoxicating him as much as the intense infatuation. Henrietta then pulled herself free from his embrace and three much younger men simultaneously approached for the prospect of a dance.

After the ball, Daniel Doyle asked Henrietta where she was staying, and she told him she would be staying in London for a week with her uncle near Shaftsbury Avenue.

"Within three days I shall bring London to a standstill for you. If I succeed, will I have won your heart?" Doyle asked dreamily.

"Perhaps," she smirked, then lifted her knuckles to Daniel's lips and he gently kissed them.

Henrietta was then escorted home by her uncle, and every man in the room sighed, just as every young woman was relieved by her departure. Nathan Kingsley saw that his friend was extremely besotted by Miss Shelbourne, and generously said: "You should have her, let's forget the wager".

And so the bet was cancelled.

Daniel Doyle and Nathan Kingsley booked into a hotel overlooking Shaftsbury Avenue. On the following morning, Doyle bought reams of paper and sheets of stamps. He wrote dozens upon dozens of letters; stacks of them, and he persuaded his good friend Mr Kingsley to do the same for the purpose of a grand master plan he was hatching. A bellboy at the hotel kept taking piles of these letters to be posted, thinking the men were just conducting business. The letter writing went on all night for two solid days. No sleep, just drinking, eating and writing, until Nathan Kingsley's fingers were crippled with writer's cramp. On the third day, something momentous took place, which would go down in the history books.

Just after dawn, a flock of 80 chimney sweeps turned up at the house next door but one from where Henrietta Shelbourne was staying. The unfortunate widow who answered the door was speechless when she saw all the sweeps. They, in turn, were indignant, saying they had been summoned to her house by a letter. Five coal wagons then turned up, followed by a fleet of furniture carts, a number of funeral hearses, and a string of hansom cabs carrying midwives, doctors, dentists and various summoned guests. Then a convoy of beer wagons arrived from the Trueman Brewery in the East End. They were followed by a wagon carrying a pipe organ and seven carters pushing loads of potatoes. Three butchers then tried to get into the packed street.

By noon, the Governor of the Bank of England had arrived, the Lord Chief Justice, the Lord Mayor of London, and the Archbishop of Canterbury. Then the crowds went berserk when the Royal Coach appeared in the congested street, because the Duke of York – who was also the Commander-in-Chief of the British Army – had been informed by mail that his most decorated and loyal officer was dying at the widow's house. Then a Naval Chief turned up, and another wave of assorted people arrived at the chaotic scene. The congestion which followed was an early form of gridlock. The horses and carts were unable to move, and the area was soon redolent with the smell of numerous piles of horse manure. The brimming thoroughfare brought the centre of the capital to a halt.

In the middle of all this pandemonium, Daniel Doyle managed to forge his way through to Henrietta Shelbourne's house to claim his prize. The girl was looking out of her uncle's window, laughing at the riot of people and police filling the streets. She waved to Doyle, and he shouted up to her over the din: "I brought London to a standstill for you, now may I have your heart?"

Henrietta giggled childishly and placed her hand across her mouth. She shouted something to the besotted middle-aged man standing pathetically amongst the jostling crowds on the pavement below. Daniel Doyle had to strain his ears to catch what she was shouting over the incessant clamour.

"I was pulling your leg!" she blithely cried, throwing her head back in delight.

A handsome young man suddenly appeared at the window and began kissing the girl's beautiful, slender neck. He too looked down at Doyle and guffawed when he saw his earnest face; disbelief and disappointment etched on its wrinkled features.

Daniel Doyle's heart was torn apart. He returned to Liverpool with Nathan Kingsley a broken man, humiliated by his own folly. A well-known hoaxer named Theodore Hook was afterwards blamed for the so-called Berners Street Hoax, but although Hook revelled in the glory, he secretly admitted to friends that he was not behind the biggest practical joke that London has ever known. No one knew the true heartache that lay behind a jest perpetrated to win a lady's heart.

The Huyton Spaceman and the Risley Robot

The following tale technically should not be included in a book of the paranormal, as it concerns the ever-enigmatic UFO phenomenon, but I am convinced that there is a paranormal aspect to some of the strange unidentified craft and their surreal occupants that have been seen in our skies.

The year 1977 was certainly the year of the UFO here in the Northwest. It was the year when lights and disc-shaped vehicles were seen in droves (what is the collective noun for UFOs?) in the skies over Cheshire, Lancashire, North Wales, Merseyside, and the Isle of Man. That same year, the terrifying, seven-foot, robotic-looking 'Kirkby Spaceman' was allegedly seen near the Yorkshire Imperial Metals plant and, not to be outdone, Huyton also had visitors from elsewhere.

On the chilly Tuesday afternoon of 22 February 1977, at 4.30pm, twelve-year-old English schoolboy, Alan Street, walked out of his home in the Huyton district of Liverpool to empty the kitchen bin into a dustbin in the garden, when he noticed something which made him stop in his tracks. A white helmeted head with strange staring eyes was protruding from the bushes at the bottom of the garden. Alan felt uneasy and somehow sensed that the thing peeping at him was unearthly. He dashed back into the house to fetch his mother. Mrs Street came out and took a look for herself and she froze in terror. A bizarre-looking entity, about nine feet in height, was hovering over the bushes at the bottom of the garden. The figure was clad in white plastic and grey metal 'armour' and the eyes on its mouthless face seemed as lifeless as the lenses on a pair of binoculars. The robotic figure had two arms and legs, but its incredible height and towering stature gave it a menacing air. The thing looked alien, other worldly and understandably, Mrs Street and her son scrambled rapidly back into the house as the mechanical giant defied gravity and floated towards them with a faint humming sound.

Once inside, Alan yanked the curtains closed as his mother telephoned the police, but as you can imagine, the emergency call was not taken too seriously. Mrs Street waited for the police to arrive to no avail, and at one point she heard the low-pitched hum and whirring sound of the sinister trespasser as it came close to the living room window. She dared to open the curtains a fraction and recoiled in horror when she saw the globular insect-like eyes staring in at her and Alan. What did it want? Where was it from? What was it, for that matter? Endless questions raced through the Huyton housewife's panic-stricken mind.

Suddenly, Mrs Street heard footsteps outside. She peeped through the window and saw that it was her neighbour, May. There was no sign of the bug-eyed robot anywhere. May hammered frantically on the door and was promptly admitted. She was visibly shaken, as she had just encountered what she described as a 'big spaceman'. The thing had floated around to the rear of Mrs Street's house, May said. Suddenly, the eerie sound of the automated humanoid grew to such intensity, that the window panes vibrated. Mrs Street told May and Alan to make a dash for it, while she tackled the suburban spaceman with a broom! Mrs Street opened the door and shouted at the figure, but it stared at her without making a move. She thrust her broom at it without evoking the slightest reaction, while May and Alan refused to make a run for it because their nerves had got the better of them.

Moments after the brave confrontation, Mrs Street watched in awe as the figure turned a perfect 180 degrees, then rose into the air and started to accelerate sideways. As it was passing over a row of garden walls, a police car arrived, and two constables witnessed the flying simulacrum's departure in total amazement. More people came forward and said they had also encountered what the media called the 'Huyton Spaceman'. Several people said the figure was seen in conjunction with a UFO that was hanging low in the sky over a local primary school. UFO investigators subsequently discovered that a boy who lived near Mrs Street had found a sparkling, golfball-sized metal globe in his garden, which had allegedly fallen from the sky. The boy's mother later threw the globe out with other rubbish. Was this curious globe perhaps the thing that the Huyton Spaceman had been searching for?

In the following year, on the night of 17 March 1978, another mechanical-looking figure was encountered at Risley by a service engineer named Ken Edwards. Edwards was driving home, and part of his route passed an atomic power plant. As he approached this plant in his van, the vehicle's headlights revealed something very unusual indeed. A silvery, seven-foot-tall, humanoid machine was galumphing down an embankment from the power plant with a robotic gait. The entity walked along with its arms outstretched, and although it was off balance on the embankment's sharp incline, it seemed to defy gravity by not toppling over. Its small globular head spun through 90 degrees, so its luminous eyes faced the oncoming van. Two pencil-thin beams of scarlet light blinked on and the laser-like shafts scanned the van and its astonished driver, while the machine continued on its way across the road. It then not only defied the laws of gravity but also the laws of physics as we understand them, because the machine walked up the steep incline and straight through a security fence that was topped with barbed wire.

The van Edwards had been travelling in spluttered to a halt as the engine stalled. He later discovered that the van's radio had been burnt out by a massive power surge, and even more mysterious, the service engineer had somehow 'lost' about thirty minutes which he could not account for. Two years after this weird experience, Ken Edwards was sadly diagnosed as having cancer, and he died in 1982. Whether or not his cancer was caused by the UFO entity at Risley will probably never be known.

The Imprint

Over the years their have been several sightings of a certain ghost in the grounds of Wavertree's Blue Coat School after dark. A few years ago a policeman told me how a Wavertree resident reported seeing a grey-haired man roaming the school playground at night. He looked as if he was searching for something because he kept looking at the ground as he walked about.

Anyway, the police arrived and found no one in the vicinity of the school. The same figure was reported twice more that night, but whenever the police investigated, they could find no trace of a trespasser. For years it looked as if the identity of the ghost of Blue Coat School would remain a mystery, until a listener to my show on Radio Merseyside enlightened me. Very recently, an old retired policeman named Arthur described the ghost to a tee; detailing the clothes it wore and exactly where it was seen. Furthermore, he then told me whose ghost people had been seeing all those years, and the tale he related was a sad one.

In the 1950s, Arthur's beat took in Smithdown Road and Church Road in Wavertree, right up past Picton Clock. One rainy night in November 1952, at around eleven o'clock, Arthur was walking this beat, when he heard what sounded like a man crying. The sound was coming from inside the grounds of the Blue Coat School. Arthur climbed over a wall and saw a man of about 50 with a mop of curly grey hair in a dark corner of the grounds. The man was kneeling down, and leaning on one hand.

Arthur slowly approached the man and asked him what the matter was, but he did not answer. In fact he seemed to be unaware of the policeman's presence. Arthur decided that the man was not really a threat, just a bit confused or possibly drunk, and he crouched down by him.

"Cold tonight isn't it?" he said.

The man turned to Arthur and nodded with an expression of infinite sadness. His eyes were red and brimming with tears. Arthur looked down and saw that the man's hand was spread over the bottom step of the four steps leading to the playground. When the man took his hand away, Arthur saw the imprint of a tiny hand in the step, obviously made by a child when wet cement had coated the step. The man said that his name was Tony, and explained that the imprint was the handprint of his daughter, Marjory. Five years ago he had been taking his six-year-old daughter to school, when she had slipped from his grip as the man had been arguing with his son. When he caught up with her she was in the playground of the Blue Coat School. She had mischievously dipped her hand in the wet cement of the new steps. Marjorie thought it was really funny, and her father managed to get her out of the school playground before anyone noticed.

Anyway, later that year, in December, Marjorie had come down with a high fever and the doctor diagnosed flu, but it turned out to be meningitis. The girl became critically ill and sadly died. In the following year, Tony's wife divorced him and he turned to alcohol in an effort to try and cope with the loss of the little girl who had been the apple of his eye. Tony's wife won custody of their son. Every now and then, Tony would stop off at the school on his way home from the pub to see and feel the imprint of his beloved Marjorie's hand on that step.

Tony never got over the loss of his daughter and the collapse of his marriage, and was found dead near Wavertree Park from alcoholic poisoning. Not long afterwards, people reported seeing his ghost in the Blue Coat playground. Today, the imprint of the little girl's hand is barely visible because the steps have been weathered, and worn down with the feet of hundreds of children.

Chatroom Ghost

Ghosts, and particularly poltergeists, can affect just about every technical appliance, from TV sets to telephones, and in recent years there has been a plethora of reports of ghosts 'possessing' personal computers. The following strange story is a case in point.

In December 1998, 13-year-old Mandy Belvedere suffered a fatal asthma attack and died in her bedroom in Austin, Texas. Mandy's asthma had been steadily worsening since 1996, and doctors had concluded that the girl was allergic to modern life. It was hypothesised that the artificial chemical additives which lace so many of our foods nowadays were having a detrimental effect on the teenager's health, but no matter which diet was tried, she would always end up fighting for her breath, and had to have an oxygen tank permanently in her room.

Another allergic reaction she had suffered resulted in scaly eczema-like patches, which would appear on the girl's face and arms. Mandy's condition dramatically curtailed her teenage social life. She had a daily home tutor, who popped in for a few hours each day. Without a doubt, her personal computer provided her with hours of fun and interaction with other teenagers, as Mandy often talked to her peers via the Excite Corporation's Internet chatrooms. She usually went under the name 'Belvedere_13' – her surname and age. Mandy had several friends in America and Europe who talked to her in *Teen Chat*, and she came across as a very witty and funny girl. Two good friends of Mandy's were Southport girls, Chloe and Emily. They were devastated when Mandy died. She was also a friend of a fourteen-year-old Aigburth boy called Justin, who had even made plans to visit the Texan girl before her tragic death.

However, shortly after Mandy's death, something bizarre happened. Mandy's screen-name, Belvedere_13, continued to appear on the screens of people exchanging messages on Excite's *Teen Chat* – Mandy's favourite Internet chatroom. When Mandy's mother was alerted, she assumed some sick hoaxer was at work, but events took a spine-chilling turn when Mrs Belvedere logged onto *Teen Chat* and challenged the person 'masquerading' as her deceased daughter. She asked Mandy to prove that she was her daughter by answering three very personal questions (which I cannot go into here).

Belvedere_13 answered all three queries in such accurate detail that Mrs Belvedere almost fainted. More and more questions were put to Belvedere_13 by the other members of Mandy's family, and each of them was answered in amazing depth.

"Oh my God! Is that you Mandy? Is it really my girl?" Mrs Belvedere sobbed as she tapped in the question.

The typed answer came back ... "Yes, Mom."

When Mrs Belvedere asked the girl how it was possible to be in a chatroom on the Internet if she was dead, Belvedere_13 failed to reply. Further questions were also met with a lack of response. The company running the chatroom was allegedly asked to try and trace the whereabouts of Belvedere_13, but they said that it was impossible.

Reports are still coming in that Belvedere_13 still chats to people at *Teen Chat* even today. If you use the chatrooms, keep an eye out for the mysterious Belvedere_13 ...

Blighted Love

On Wavertree's Church Road, there is a church called the Holy Trinity, which dates from 1794. Facing this church, on the other side of the road, there are three ancient stone steps known locally as the mounting stone. From the late 1790s, churchgoers used to stand on these steps to mount their horses.

Around 1800, a love affair began on those exact stone steps. Catherine Mayfield, the 22-year-old daughter of a local merchant named Alfred Mayfield, left Holy Trinity, and returned to her horse, which was tethered by a row of posts on Church Road. Her suitor, Joshua Quiller, a hard-headed businessman who owned paper factories in Liverpool and London, was neglecting Catherine as usual and talking shop with several other businessmen who had just left the church service. Catherine stood on the mounting stone, but the horse trotted off before she could mount it and she clung awkwardly to its mane and saddle, with one foot caught in the stirrup. A youth of about eighteen suddenly appeared and seized the horse's reins and steadied her. He brought her back to the mounting steps, and Catherine was able to get into the saddle with some dignity. She thanked the boy, who had a mop of black curly hair and an attractive, friendly face, neither of which was lost on Catherine. He smiled at her and then walked away, but it was one of those examples of love at first sight that you hear about. In those brief moments, something connected between them.

Catherine made secret enquiries about the youth, and discovered that he was a local orphan named Joel. He had been raised by a Jewish couple who gave him the name, but he ended up running away from home and had been living rough on the streets of Liverpool. He had been in trouble for hunting wood pigeons and other fowl on the various estates of Wavertree. In short, he was a vagabond. But, when Jill's in love with Jack, his pockmarks seem like dimples, and so a well-to-do lady saw beyond the grimy image of the young vagrant, and she fell rapidly in love with him.

She persuaded her father, Alfred, to hire Joel to work on the sprawling acres of the family homestead near what is now Menlove Avenue. That summer, Catherine Mayfield started a love affair with Joel that was somewhat absurd. The young man had a limited vocabulary and was almost slow-witted, and yet Catherine ignored his shortcomings and only noticed his gentle side. He collected a rainbow arrangement of wild flowers for her, and on the summer nights, the two of them would sit hidden away under an old oak tree, gazing at the Milky Way and the occasional shooting star. Joel was in tune with nature, unlike Catherine's suitor, Joshua Quiller, who spoke about nothing but money.

In August, Catherine discovered that she was pregnant with Joel's child, and she visited an old friend of the family named Mrs Plaistow for advice. Mrs Plaistow unfortunately revealed Catherine's secret to a relative, and within a few days, the shocking news of the pregnancy reached the ears of Joshua Quiller. He was devastated and quickly turned to drink, but did not tell anyone about his sweetheart's infidelity and chose not to reveal to his beloved that he knew the awful truth. He bought an expensive wedding ring, and visited Catherine late one night and asked for her hand in marriage.

She gratefully accepted, deciding to pass off the child she was carrying as Joshua's. Catherine Quiller, as she now became, moved to London with her husband, who had purchased an enormous property on Hampstead Heath. In an apparent show of generosity, Joel was invited down to London to work on the estate by Joshua Quiller.

One day, Joel went missing without warning, and Catherine was devastated at the disappearance, as she still had strong feelings for him and, of course, was bearing his child. She asked her husband if he knew what had become of the young man, but Joshua simply shook his head. Catherine suspected that her husband did know something about Joel's absence, and more than likely had something to do with it.

On the following day, Catherine and Joshua were travelling across the old London Bridge in a carriage, when the vehicle was forced to a halt because of the huge crowds blocking the bridge. Joshua stepped out of the carriage to see what was causing the disturbance. The crowds were looking over the bridge at something below. Curiosity got the better of Catherine, and she too left the carriage to see what was happening.

One of the onlookers informed her that a pirate had been chained to the walls below London Bridge. The tide was coming in and soon the pirate would be drowned. Catherine shuddered at the thought, although it was a common enough spectacle in those days. She peeped over the bridge only to see Joel shackled and chained to the bridge wall, the waves already lapping round his neck. Nauseous with shock, she almost passed out. Joshua slipped an arm around her and chuckled, gloatingly admitting that he had framed the youth and bribed the authorities to state that Joel had been found guilty of piracy. Catherine demanded to know why he had done such a cruel thing, and he jabbed at her stomach and vindictively hissed:

"That child is not mine; it is his!"

Catherine turned from him and dashed through the crowd, and scrambled over the wall before anyone could stop her. There was a great commotion as she dropped into the murky freezing waters of the Thames below. Witnesses said that Catherine swam to Joel, and tried desperately to pull off the manacles, but the water rose relentlessly until it covered his head. Catherine took deep gulps of air and dived under the water to blow the air into her drowning lover's mouth, but it was useless, and tragically, they both died, holding hands. She died from shock and hypothermia from the freezing Thames.

There is a gruesome footnote to this story. Joshua Quiller was buried in Highgate Cemetery, and in 1960, his grave had to be exhumed because of subsidence. His coffin had been split open by the strong root of a yew tree which had coiled itself around the corpse's neck. The end of the root appeared to come out of the mouth, looking as if Quiller's tongue had wrapped itself around his neck.

The story of Catherine and Joel later reached the ears of Emily Bronte, and she loosely based Heathcliff – a Liverpool waif – on the character of Joel.

The Karmic Wheel

In Victorian times, Joseph Wigglesworth, a man who had lost both his legs in an accident at the age of thirteen in 1830, used to sit on a sort of cart on Pudsey Street. Of course, there was no welfare state at that time, so Joe had to resort to playing a penny whistle to earn a few bob. His loyal mongrel dog, Sandy, was his only real friend, and she used to perform tricks at a signal from Joe. The financial returns from these activities was meagre, and Joe would end up with nothing more than a few pennies and farthings in his cap. He was very independent though, and somehow scraped enough money for his weekly rent. He lived in a tiny hovel in Bridport Street.

On a cold February morning in 1860, a weeping rain fell from a slate-grey sky. Joe was begging on the corner of Lime Street and Pudsey Street, when two finely dressed men in top hats stood before him. One of them began to talk about him in an offensive manner. They saw the single penny in his cap, and they watched with bemused grins as Sandy stood on her hind legs and raised her front paws in a begging gesture.

The dog had a little comical hat strapped on her head.

One of the men, Edward Sims, a wealthy cotton broker, asked Joseph if his dog was for sale, and he produced a guinea, and flipped it about in his hand, trying to tempt him. Joe was starving, but he loved Sandy. He had raised her from her days as an abandoned pup.

"No, she isn't for sale, sir."

Edward Sims became furious, and his colleague, Ferguson Bright, laughed and held out his hand. Edward Sims shuffled away and swore at the street beggar. Mr Bright explained: "My friend claimed he could buy that old dog of yours, but he lost the wager."

On the following day, Joe was once again begging on the street, when Edward Sims turned up with a policeman.

"That is the accursed animal that attacked me, constable," lied the top-hatted Sims, pointing at Sandy with his cane. "It snapped at my heel on this beggar's orders, simply because I refused to give him money."

But the policeman knew old Joseph Wigglesworth well.

"I doubt that, sir," he replied. "That dog is no danger to the public. I pass here regularly on my beat, and the animal is a very peaceable creature."

Edward Sims flew into a rage and said that if the dog was not destroyed, he would see the constable's superiors. The policeman had no choice, so he stroked Sandy and picked her up. Old Joe cried out pitifully: "She's all I have in the world, please don't take her."

The policeman walked off to the police station holding Sandy, who was still wearing her little hat. The dog yelped and looked back at its master, who was in tears. Edward Sims accompanied the policeman to the station to make sure that the necessary form was filled in for the dog's destruction.

Joseph Wigglesworth was unable to raise a tune from his old penny whistle, and he lay there with his head bowed, scalding tears streaming down his face.

People passing by who had not seen what had happened, thought it was just a cheap gimmick. They could not know that the tears were real. As darkness fell, Joseph sadly made his way back to his room. At one o'clock in the morning, he heard a scratching sound at the door. He used his hands to pull himself to the door and reached up to the handle. As soon as he had released the handle, the flew door open and in dashed Sandy in a hysterical state. She licked Joe's face and danced around him yapping with excitement. She had somehow escaped from the yard of the police station.

On the following morning, Joe set himself up near London Road, instead of on his usual patch, because he was terrified of another encounter with Edward Sims. But later that day, Sims turned up once more, and menacingly pointed his cane at the dog, and again threatened to have it destroyed. However, on this occasion, Sim's colleague Ferguson Bright, turned up and intervened. He argued that Sims was just a bad sportsman who was being mean-spirited to the beggar because he had lost a wager. An altercation ensued, and Mr Bright said that if Sims bothered Joe again, he would impart certain information regarding his financial dealings to the authorities. That did the trick, and Sims never bothered Joe again.

A year later, Sims himself ended up as a cripple, when he was run down by a carriage in Edinburgh and his left leg had to be amputated below the knee. Not long afterwards, the Karmic wheel of Fate turned yet again, and Sims lost a fortune in a disastrous business venture.

Sandy died peacefully in her sleep five years later, and Joseph Wigglesworth begged on the streets of Liverpool until he died of bronchitis in 1911, aged 94.

The Kensington Banshee

In the 1950s – especially during the summer evenings – it was not unusual to see neighbouring families sitting on their doorsteps, or bringing out chairs, gossiping over cups of tea and cigarettes. They usually had their children playing round them, and they could chatter away until long after midnight, especially when the children did not have to get up for school the next day.

This was the scene in 1959 at a certain street in the Kensington district of Liverpool. Two families, the McCabes and the Joneses, lived next door to one another, and one close July evening at nine o'clock, Mrs Jones came out of her house with her curlers in and sat on her chair. Her daughters brought their mother a bowl of warm water to soak her tired feet, and a little fold-up table upon which they laid a teapot, a jug of milk, cups, a bowl of sugar and so on. Then Mrs Jones's mother came out with a deckchair and pillow, and positioned herself by the bay window. Minutes later, Mr and Mrs McCabe did the same on the adjoining doorstep. Mr McCabe came out in his string vest with two chairs, followed by his wife. She had sandwiches, a jar of pickled onions and a large bowl of blackcurrant jelly. Her little son sat on her knee, and her two daughters, Nora and Joan, sat on the ledge of the bay window wearing their nightdresses and slippers. Then someone let Terry, the little Jack Russell out. He ambled about the street and watched a few of the audacious cats slouching about.

The timing and atmosphere were perfect. It was time for a good all-nighter sort of 'jangle', and the Joneses and the McCabes set about discussing everyone's business in the street. They spent a good forty minutes talking about the comings and goings of the new family who had moved into Number 12 – the Ryans, a large Irish family. Mrs Jones and Mr McCabe complained that the Ryans were always arguing and drunk, and seemed to have half of Ireland in their house. And they whispered that the young girl was not married to the man who had made her pregnant.

Anyway, this gossip was still going on at almost one o'clock in the morning, when suddenly, the Joneses and the McCabes heard someone crying. The little Jack Russell, Terry, came hurtling down the road and bolted straight into the house. He was so terrified that he ran straight into the vestibule door and yelped with pain. Then Joan McCabe tapped her mother on the shoulder and gestured down the road.

"Mum! Look at this old woman."

Mrs Jones's old mother peered down the street.

"Who is it?" she asked.

"Say nothing, mam," said Mrs Jones, folding her arms in disapproval.

A woman was staggering drunkenly down the street, stopping every now and then. She was dressed completely in black and her long hair covered her face. The odd-looking woman stopped right in front of the Joneses and McCabes, and Mrs McCabe finally said: "Are you alright, love?"

The figure said nothing. It moved on down the street towards Number 12, where the Ryans lived. Fourteen-year-old Nora went to follow the weird looking woman, but was shocked to see that she had vanished. A moment later, an elderly man came down the street. It was Mr Ryan, the head of the Irish family who had just moved into the street. When he saw the Joneses and the McCabes sitting on their doorsteps, he stopped and surveyed the scene.

"Who's having a jamboree at this hour?" he smiled, with his hands on his hips – the jovial Irishman obviously approved of the mini street party.

"Hey, one of your lot just passed us Mr Ryan. She was in tears," said Mrs McCabe.

"Couldn't have been one of ours," said Mr Ryan, puzzled, "they're all in bed. They have to work in the morning you see."

"Well, she went towards your house," said Mrs Jones.

"Wouldn't be my sister May? Small woman with brown hair?"

"No, this woman was old, all in black. Her hair was grey, almost white. It was hanging down in front of her face."

Mr Ryan's smile froze. He made the sign of the cross.

"Sweet Jesus," he said, almost inaudibly.

The Joneses and the McCabes were intrigued. They loved a mystery.

"You just saw a banshee," said Mr Ryan.

"A banshee?" laughed Mrs Jones uneasily.

"As true as you're all sitting there, it's a banshee. There's going to be a death tonight." As he walked away, fumbling for his front door key, he muttered, "God Almighty," over and over again.

Little Norah ran after Mr Ryan and tapped him on the shoulder. The Irishman jumped with fright.

"Mr Ryan, will someone really die?" she asked.

Mr Ryan nodded with a deadpan face.

"Now, how can I explain it, child?" he said, obviously worried that he was going to upset her. "The person who didn't hear or see the banshee in those two families will pass away."

Norah ran back and told her mother and Mrs Jones what Mr Ryan had said.

"He's drunk," said Mr McCabe dismissively. "Don't listen to him, he's only trying to frighten you."

But deep down Mr McCabe felt very uneasy, because he had been the only one amongst them who had not seen the banshee. On the following morning, Mr McCabe was found dead in his bed. He had died in his sleep during the night.

Last Warlock in Wales

At the outset of World War Two in 1939, one million children were evacuated from the cities and towns of Britain. In Liverpool, two children, 13-year-old Peter Raleigh and his 11-year-old sister, Maureen, of Sackville Street in Everton, were sent to the relative safety of Gresford in Wales. Peter and Maureen, now in their seventies, told me that although these events took place over 62 years ago, to them it seems like only yesterday.

Peter and Maureen were billeted to the home of a rather strange Welsh family. To the two Liverpool evacuees, Mr and Mrs Shuker, and their 25-year-old daughter, Olwyn, seemed like people from some bygone age; all three dressed quaintly in dark Victorian-looking clothes. The living room of their granite cottage was dimly lit with a low wattage bulb and candles. The only modern item in the place was a crackly old radio. Mr Shuker looked about 65, and had a shock of white hair. His wife was small and round with rosy cheeks, and seemed to have a perpetual grin on her face. Olwyn was very docile looking and never uttered a word, except to the big, black, overweight cat, Chester. This cat did not take to the Raleigh children, and kept hissing at them and arching its back.

The children were shown their bedroom, which was little more than a tiny attic with a steeply sloping roof and a window under the eaves. Maureen opened the window and her eyes lit up, because, directly outside was an old apple tree and a branch holding big red apples was within easy reach. The children leaned out and grabbed a few. Fruit was a rare luxury in those times.

Mr Shuker took the children to the village sweetshop on the day of their arrival, and he struck them as being rather childish. Peter thought he was funny but little Maureen considered him just plain silly. As they were returning from the shop, Mr Shuker said, "Watch this children," and he pointed to a policeman who was walking along ahead of them. Mr Shuker adjusted his gait so that he was walking in step with the village constable in front of him. Peter giggled, and he also fell into step behind him. Maureen blushed with embarrassment and looked about to see if anyone was watching. Mr Shuker walked in perfect synchronisation with the bobby, then all of a sudden, the old man pretended to trip, and at that exact moment, the policeman fell over.

"How did you do that?" Peter inquired, with a look of devilish amazement.

Mr Shuker grinned like a mischievous child and said, "Resonance!" Without explaining what this meant, he walked on and helped the baffled policeman up.

On another occasion, in the following year, Mrs Shuker suddenly went to the window and looked up at the night sky. She said that German planes were on the way. About twenty minutes later, the

59

unmistakable low droning sound of enemy bombers could be heard in the skies. They were on their way to bomb Liverpool. Maureen thought it was creepy how Mrs Shuker had known about the planes before anyone else could hear them.

On another occasion, Maureen passed Olwyn Shuker's bedroom, and, seeing that her door was open, she peeped in. Olwyn had two weird-looking dolls in her hand, and she was muttering something in Welsh. Maureen watched, fascinated, as Olwyn cut off a long lock of her hair. The girl then used the hair strands to bind the two effigies together. Olwyn's cat suddenly mewed shrilly, and she caught the Liverpool girl looking in at her. The young Welsh woman told Maureen that it was rude to spy on people like that. All the same, she invited the girl in and showed her the creepy effigies, which were made from clay. Olwyn said they represented herself and a man in the village she was in love with. The effigies bound with hair were part of an elaborate love spell to make the man fall for her. Maureen was amazed when, a short time later, she saw plain-faced Olwyn linking arms with a handsome young man in the village.

The most startling revelation came one Sunday when Maureen finally asked Mr Shuker to his face if he was some sort of witch. His answer astounded her. He replied that he was a warlock, the last warlock in Wales. Maureen and Peter were enthralled as Mr Shuker showed them his wardrobe. There, among the old garments, a long black silken gown was hanging. This gown was adorned with strange symbols, stars, crescents and so on. It was obviously a magician's robe. There was also a strange pointed black cap, and in a corner of the wardrobe, what looked like a quiver of arrows. Mr Shuker explained that these were consecrated wands made of rowan: magic wands.

Something caught Peter's eye and he asked what the large yellow chunk of glass he could see in the wardrobe was. Mr Shuker picked it up and told them it was polished amber and took it downstairs where he rubbed it with a black cloth, set it in front of the table and drew the curtains. A candle was lit, and Mr Shuker put his elbows on the table and stared intently at the amber. He suddenly started to shake, his face contorted, and tears rolled down his face. He threw a black cloth over the amber, then turned and looked at the children, as if he wanted to break bad news to them, but said nothing.

When the time came for the evacuees to go home, having said goodbye to Mrs Shuker and Olwyn, Mr Shuker walked with them to the train station at Wrexham, and it started to rain heavily. Peter put on his school cap and Maureen suddenly began to fret when she realised that she had left her little umbrella.

"Don't worry, you won't get wet," said Mr Shuker, enigmatically. And they didn't; the rain seemed to fall all around them, but not on them. He hugged the children at the station and tears streamed down his cheeks as he waved to them from the platform. When the children returned home, they were devastated to learn that their Auntie Joan had been killed during the Blitz.

This had happened on the very same night that Mr Shuker had cried after gazing into the piece of amber. Had he seen Joan's death in the amber? Was this why he had been so upset?

Even more mysteriously, when Maureen went up into her bedroom, she found the umbrella she had left in the Shuker's cottage lying on her bed.

One for Sorrow

In August 1985, Tina, a 40-year-old Liverpool woman was due to travel to Manchester Airport to board a British Airways Boeing 737, which was bound for Corfu. Tina had never flown before, and was quite nervous. Her best friend, Beryl, told her there was nothing to flying, and that it was safer than crossing the road. Anyway, Beryl would be going to Corfu with her, so she would reassure her and be there for her during the flight. Beryl had just moved to Prescot, and the plan was for Tina to get a taxi from her Wavertree home to Beryl's house, then the two women would get a taxi to Manchester Airport. The flight to Corfu was due to depart at 7am, so Beryl told Tina to get to her house at around five in the morning, then they would travel to Manchester down the M62.

Tina was a nervous wreck, and the night before the flight, she got into bed at nine o'clock, but was unable to sleep. Her husband, Ron, was a security guard, and he was on a night shift from midnight until eight in the morning. He had decided not to go with Tina to Corfu. He gave Tina half a sleeping tablet and told her to relax, she would have a great time. Tina set the alarm clock for 4am, and also told Ron to ring her at four in the morning in case she overslept.

The sleeping tablet soon took effect, and Tina drifted off into a deep sleep. She had a peculiar dream that night. She dreamt that her husband

and Beryl were kissing each other, and throughout the dream, she could see a magpie flying about the place. It was very surreal. At half past three in the morning, Tina woke up, and got the shock of her life. It had been a warm August night, so she had left the top window open, and a magpie had flown into the bedroom. This was obviously strange because magpies do not usually appear until around dawn, and it was still dark at half past three. Tina was terrified of birds to the point of phobia and now, here was a huge magpie screeching and fluttering over her bed. With a shudder of revulsion she ducked down under the covers. Then suddenly the room fell silent. After listening intently for a time, Tina peeped warily over the covers. The room was very dark, and she squinted as her eyes adjusted to it. Then she saw the magpie. It was perched on top of the alarm clock, and it was watching her. Tina thought she must be dreaming, and felt very drowsy through the soporific effects of the sleeping tablet. She turned away from the magpie and, despite herself, sank into a deep sleep again.

When Tina woke up again, harsh morning sunlight was flooding into the room. She looked in panic at the alarm clock. The time was half past eight in the morning. She leapt out of bed. She examined the clock – the tiny button on the top of the alarm clock had been pushed down.

So that was why the alarm had not sounded. Yet she distinctly remembered pulling that button up to enable the alarm. Then, as she grew more awake, she recalled the strange magpie which had landed on the clock. She looked over at the window; it was open. She had not been dreaming. She swore and cursed Ron. Why had he not phoned to wake her up? She picked up the telephone receiver and found that the line was dead. Tina later noticed a British Telecom van outside the house. Children in the area had vandalised the telephone junction box. All the lines in the street were out of order.

Tina made herself a cup of tea and turned on the radio. She heard on the news that there had been an air disaster at Manchester Airport. A fire had broken out in the port engine of a Boeing 737 as it had been taking off – bound for Corfu! The plane was ablaze on the taxiway. Fifty-five people had died in the tragic inferno. Tina burst into tears, because she assumed that Beryl had been on the plane. Beryl had warned her that she would go to Corfu with or without her.

Tina ran to a neighbour's house and the woman there held her as she sobbed bitterly. Suddenly, the two women looked out of the window as footsteps approached. Tina's husband Ron was coming down the road with Beryl. They went next door. Tina ran out, and was just about to greet them but when she reached the path, she was stunned by the sight that greeted her eyes. Beryl and Ron were standing in the hallway of her home, and they were locked in a passionate embrace. It was just like the image in Tina' dream.

That morning, Beryl had also overslept, after Tina's husband had spent the night with her. They had surmised that Tina had perished in the air disaster, because Ron had telephoned a friend who was a baggage handler at Manchester Airport and told him that he was unable to get through to the officials at the Airport. The baggage handler said the situation was chaotic, but also that he had handled Tina's baggage, and had even talked to her. This baggage handler had obviously been mistaken.

When Beryl and Ron were caught kissing in the hallway, they were shocked to say the least. Ron claimed he had been merely comforting Tina's best friend, that was all. But Tina saw through this and later divorced her unfaithful husband. To this day, she often wonders about the strange magpie which saved her life – and revealed her husband to be an adulterer.

Tunnel Vision

The following unusual story was related to me a few years ago, and has been backed up by the testimony of doctors and hospital medical staff whom I have contacted and interviewed.

In 1997, a 45-year-old Bootle man, Stephen Lodge, heard himself being pronounced dead at the scene of a car crash in Greater Manchester. Then he noticed a faint buzzing noise and a strange harmony of voices singing. He was gradually losing the feeling in his body, and the sensation of being trapped in the wreckage of his car slowly faded. Stephen was suddenly hurtling headfirst down a dark tunnel. This tunnel seemed immense, and at the end of it there was a beautiful light which looked like the sun, yet it did not hurt his eyes.

This amazing incident was taking place at about five minutes past three in the afternoon.

At that exact time, a 40-year-old woman in Speke named Susan, was getting ready to pick her children up from school when she suddenly suffered a severe asthma attack in the kitchen. The attack was so bad that she started to choke, and then collapsed on the floor. She tried to shout for help, but could not get the words out of her constricted throat. She then suffered a respiratory arrest. The kitchen went dark, and suddenly she heard what she described as the roaring sound of a gale force wind. Susan found herself floating along a vast tunnel, heading towards a brilliant light. She looked to her right and saw the silhouette of a stranger. It was a man. He gazed at her with an expression of bewilderment and apprehension, and she suddenly said to him: "I have to pick the children up".

She reached out to the man, and he reached out for her. They were both frightened, and were soon holding hands as they headed towards this unknown golden light source. They both heard a rhythmic sound, similar to waves breaking on the shore. Suddenly, they passed through a bright glare, and simultaneously experienced an amazing feeling of joy and optimism. They had an awareness that death was nonsense, that it was the living who were in a state of death, and the pair felt as if they were now truly living.

They passed through a warm luminous glow, and found themselves in a beautiful landscape of mountains and green fields on a summer's day. A crowd of people, some dressed in silvery blue, and others in pure white, greeted the couple. Some were strangers and others, deceased relatives. A man stepped forward and addressed the newly arrived migrant: "Stephen, please go back. Maureen needs you". Stephen suddenly recognised the man: it was his uncle Jim.

However, Jim appeared much younger, and his hair was dark. It had been snow white when he died six years before. Stephen did not recognise any of the other people. He tried to look behind them at the beautiful picturesque scenery, but the people smiled and crowded together to block his view. A black man seemed to know something, and he shook his head as he looked at Stephen.

The other new arrival, Susan, was embracing her mother, who had died ten years before. Susan was crying and hugging her. Another woman came forward and kissed Susan. It was her grandmother who had died way back in the late 1970s, yet she looked rejuvenated.

Stephen could hear the two women telling Susan that she would have to go back to her two children. Susan kept crying and clinging onto her mother and her gran, but they laughed and wiped her tears. They reassuringly told her not to be silly, because they would still be waiting when she came back. Stephen shook hands with his uncle, and then hugged him, because he somehow knew that he would not be staying. Within a heartbeat, Stephen and Susan were travelling backwards, tumbling back down the mysterious tunnel which had brought them to some plane of existence which exists beyond death.

Stephen held Susan's hand tightly as they sped faster and faster, and they both heard a jumble of sounds. Then Stephen felt Susan's small hand slip from his grip and he woke up and saw white squares. It was the ceiling of a hospital. He later learned that minutes after he had been pronounced dead, his heart had started to beat erratically. He was resuscitated and then taken to hospital. Well, Stephen made a full recovery, and slowly recalled the near death journey he had experienced, and the woman he had met in the tunnel of light. He remembered that her name had been Susan.

Susan woke up in an ambulance after a neighbour happened to call round and looked through the kitchen window and saw her lying on the floor. She made a full recovery, even though her heart had stopped for almost two minutes. When Susan saw her two little children, a six-year-old girl and eight-year-old boy, she cried and hugged them.

Nine months later, Stephen was at a wedding at a church in Speke when he spotted Susan sitting with his cousin in the church. He recognised her instantly. Coming out of the church she also recognised him and was really stunned. They compared their experiences, and Susan was amazed when Stephen accurately described her late mother and grandmother. Susan remembered that Stephen had been talking with a man and shaking his hand. At that time, Susan had been dating Stephen's cousin, but she started seeing Stephen instead, and I believe they later decided to live together. It was a love that had been born through a meeting in the tunnel of light.

Mersey Mermaid

Over 70 per cent of the Earth is covered in water, and many scientists believe that all life on this planet originated in the sea. When a human being is developing in the womb, the foetus actually grows a set of gills and a tail at one point, and biologists think this is an indication of the early aquatic origins of mankind. Many babies are born through waterbirth nowadays, because a newborn baby breathes amniotic fluid in the womb until it is born, and the shock of breathing in air makes the child cry. You may have also seen how new born babies can instinctively swim under water. Taken further, this may throw some light on why humans like to holiday on beaches by the seaside, and why mankind has always been fascinated by water and the exploration of the sea. Now, could there be a missing link between ourselves and sea creatures? The following strange story suggests that there might be.

In 1848, Richard Mattaign, a 25-year-old Liverpool sailor, boarded a huge ship called the *Ocean Monarch* at Liverpool. The ship was bound for the United States, but when she was passing within six miles of the Great Orme, off the coast of North Wales, tragedy struck. An immigrant passenger aboard the *Ocean Monarch* mistook a ventilator for a chimney, and lit a fire which soon spread throughout the ship. People panicked and dozens crawled along the bowsprit at the front of the ship to escape the flames, while others were trapped in various parts of the ship and burned to death. Some were forced to jump into the raging sea. Richard Mattaign staggered onto the deck suffering from smoke inhalation, then fell over the ship's rail into the sea.

Hundreds perished in the tragedy. A survivor, Richard Mattaign woke to see a full moon in the sky. He felt weak, and he looked around and found himself being pulled along in the waves. A woman with a very pale complexion and long black hair had her arms under his arms, and she was swimming along with him through the waves. Richard Mattaign thought he was hallucinating and passed out. When he regained consciousness, he found himself on the beach at Hoylake and standing over him was a naked woman – the same woman with the pallid face who had rescued him from the sea. It was a sultry August night, and Mattaign did not feel at all cold. He felt weaker than he had ever felt in his life, but he managed to stagger to his feet. As he did so, the strange woman backed away from him, then ran silently in the moonlight down the beach to the sea.

"No, wait, who are you?" cried Mattaign, his thin voice dying on the breeze, and he watched as the woman walked into the sea. She kept walking until her head dipped under the waves. Richard Mattaign was convinced that he had been rescued from the shipwreck by a mermaid, but when he told people about his experiences, they looked at him strangely and obviously thought that the whole episode had been so traumatic that it had unhinged him.

The only person who believed Mattaign was an old sailor named O'Connell, because he said he had seen what he called, 'the people of the sea' when he lived near Black Rock, off the coast of Leasowe. The legend of the Black Rock mermaid goes back into the mists of time, and for hundreds of years, people have claimed to have heard the sound of a submerged bell ringing beneath the waves. It is said by some to be the bell of a church that sank in mediaeval times.

After he had physically recovered from his ordeal, Mattaign journeyed to Leasowe and secured a job there, but his behaviour became increasingly odd. He claimed that he had met the mermaid who had saved him as he was bathing in the sea. Strangely enough, several other people did see him on several occasions with a woman, who would always vanish when they drew near. Mattaign told anyone who would listen that the mermaid was guarded by a seal and a long swordfish, which had attacked him until the woman of the deep called it off. This swordfish apparently had a blue diamond shape between its eyes.

Mattaign ended up in the old sailors' home, where he often related tales about the merfolk. He told how one day he saw a cloudy disturbance in the water, and three men came out of the waves and took the mermaid back to depths of the sea, and he never saw her again.

Just before Mattaign died he asked to be buried at sea, so that he could be reunited with the mermaid he loved, but his wishes were ignored and he was put in a pauper's grave. Strangely enough, a month after he died, a huge swordfish was caught near Perch Rock. It had a distinctive blue diamond-shaped blaze pattern between its eyes. Possibly this was a coincidence, and perhaps Mattaign invented his tales of the mermaid. Possibly not ...

Ghost Train

In the late 1960s, a very intriguing but terrifying supernatural incident took place in the Wavertree area of Liverpool.

There used to be a row of terraced houses off Pigue Lane in Wavertree, but they have now been demolished; the Wavertree Nursing Home and the Greenacres estate now stand on the location. One summer night in May 1968 or 1969, a woman called Mrs Crowther was doing the washing up in her kitchen sink when a dark figure walked past the window. The stranger wore a black cap of some sort, and was carrying a long iron bar. Mrs Crowther turned off the kitchen light and looked out into her yard. The man had vanished, but another neighbour saw the same man on the following night. He felt that the man in black looked like a railway worker of some sort; he could tell by the style of his cap. Also, the bar which the man was carrying was the same type of bar used by the shunter men to undo railway line couplings. But this did not make sense because the railway was quite a long distance away from the houses.

Then one night, a week later, a family in the same street watched their chandelier start to sway dramatically. Then they heard a deep, thunderous rumbling, which caused the fabric of the house to shudder. Ornamental plates clattered off the walls with the vibration and the family dog started to howl. Everyone in the street came rushing out of their houses, thinking it must be an earthquake. It soon came to light that the mysterious disturbance had started at one end of the street and had gradually worked its way through each house in turn, like a wave.

But worse was yet to come. On the following Friday, at precisely midnight, a Mrs Richardson was sitting on her young son's bed, telling him a story because he could not get to sleep, when she heard a distant roar, and it seemed to be coming in her direction. It sounded like a heavy rumble, and the young lad clutched the bedclothes, petrified. He clung onto his mother, and for a moment she thought a jetplane was about to crash into the house. The noise grew louder and louder, and suddenly it was passing through the downstairs part of the house. Mrs Richardson prayed that the place would not collapse, because it felt as if the floor was sinking. Then an ear-splitting whistle sounded; like the whistle of a steam train. Seconds later, the whistle ceased and the deep rumbling suddenly stopped.

Mrs Richardson rushed downstairs with her son hanging onto her dress. She found the place in total disarray. The table had moved towards the window, an armchair was overturned, and stranger still, the walls and the windows were dripping with condensation, and a burning , sooty smell filled the air.

It was the same story next door, and also a few doors down. Just one house in the middle had remained unaffected. The end terraced house was occupied by an uncle and nephew, and they both said that they had seen an apparition of a solid-looking steam train emerge from the last house and vanish with a thunderous flash into the night at the end of Pigue Lane. A vast plume of steam had been blossoming from its funnel and the train had a huge glowing lantern on it.

That same eventful night, an old railway worker named Mr Adamson died in his sleep. The coroner reported the time of death as being around midnight, when the phantom twelve o'clock train had allegedly passed through the row of terraces. Some of the more superstitious residents thought that perhaps the ghost train had come to pick up the dead railway worker on his last journey.

People living across the street heard nothing and claimed it was just a ghost story that had got out of hand, but the residents who experienced the phenomenon rigorously defended their claims.

Millionaire Tramp

In 1965 a 20-year-old man named Jimmy Hughes left his Liverpool home in Scotland Road to get away from his drunken father. His mother had died a few years before, and Jimmy had been heartbroken because she had always encouraged him and spoiled him, even though she was poor, and she had compensated for his drunken father. So his childhood had been full of love.

Anyway, Jimmy Hughes moved into a bedsit in the Dingle. He found himself a job in the YMCA on Mount Pleasant, working in the kitchen, mopping floors, making beds, and cleaning tables in the dining area. He was a really hard worker. One evening he went to a place called the Sink Club on Hardman Street, because it only cost two-and-six to get in the place. And it was there that he met a beautiful blonde-haired girl from Thingwall, on the Wirral. Her name was Penny Johnson, and from the way she spoke and her manners, Jimmy could tell that she was middle-class. Even so, Jimmy and Penny really hit it off, and they ended up leaving the club together.

The couple hailed a taxi which took them to a house on Ullet Road, where Penny was staying for a few days with her cousin. Unknown to her, Jimmy was so 'skint', that he walked home in the pouring rain to his dingy bedsit in the Dingle, but he did not care because he was in love. The only problem was that he had told Penny that he owned his own garage on Roscoe Street, to impress her. He was too proud to admit to working in the 'YM' as they called the YMCA in those days.

On top of all that, Penny had suggested going on a date to a restaurant during the following week, when she would be staying at her cousin's again. Jimmy had suggested Reece's Grill Room in Clayton Square; he wanted to give Penny a great night out, so he asked a few people for a loan, but no one would lend him anything.

On the following day, disaster struck. Jimmy was cleaning the YMCA kitchen when he saw an amusing sight. Several rows of cakes, pies and sausage rolls had been laid out on a table, ready to go in a display cabinet in the canteen. Suddenly, a hand emerged from under the tablecloth and felt around for a cake, then grabbed it and Jimmy drew a few people's attention to the funny spectacle. Someone was obviously hiding under the table, stealing the cakes and sausage rolls. The manager could not see the funny side and lifted the tablecloth to reveal an old man in a dirty dufflecoat, squatting underneath with crumbs all over his beard. The manager recognised him as an old tramp who had been seen around the place recently. The tramp's name was believed to be Cassidy and some people called him Grandad. That was all that was known about him.

The manager told the vagrant to leave, but he refused, so the police were called. In a whisper, Jimmy Hughes advised him to disappear before they arrived. The tramp smiled at him. There was something in his eyes which set him apart from the usual meth-soaked tramps of the streets. Something melancholic and intelligent flickered in the old man's China blue eyes. There was a lot of hurt in those eyes, but who had inflicted the pain, and what sad history lay within remained a mystery.

When the manager saw Jimmy Hughes letting the tramp escape via the staff door he was furious,

"That's it, Mr Hughes, you're sacked! Instant dismissal," he barked.

Jimmy was devastated. It was Thursday – pay day – and he would not be getting his wages now. How on earth could he take Penny out? He felt sick at heart. It was at this point that something unbelievable happened. As Jimmy Hughes was dejectedly putting on his coat, the tramp came back in the YMCA through the staff door. In a well-spoken voice, reminiscent of James Mason, he said to Jimmy: "I'm sorry. I'm sorry they gave you the sack because you helped me."

"Oh, leave it out, it's OK," said Jimmy, trying to raise a smile, but still feeling sick inside.

The tramp reached into his pocket and took out an old leather wallet. His grimy fingers flipped through a wad of crisp banknotes and offered them to Jimmy, who was struck dumb when he realised what they were. The notes were of denominations he had never even seen before, in shades of purple and red. They were £100 notes. The tramp had just given him about ten of these notes, and he still had a wad of them in his wallet.

"You're a good man," said Cassidy, who then promptly left before Jimmy could ask any questions.

Jimmy Hughes chased after him and shouted down the street, but the tramp vanished into the crowds. Jimmy later heard that the tramp was supposed to have been a millionaire who chose to live as a hobo in Liverpool. A newsagent in Mount Pleasant said he apparently had been a tycoon who had suffered a breakdown over a failed romance, and that he had chosen to live on the streets in an attempt to forget her. He was a common figure in the hostel in Shaw Street.

Oh, by the way, Jimmy and Penny did have their date that night. They later married, and now live on the Isle of Man.

The Man Who Reported His Own Murder

This is a very strange tale that was related to me by an elderly listener to my half-hour slot on BBC Radio Merseyside. The policeman in the tale was her own father, and she even backed her story up with photographs and documents that were later shown to me. Anyway, here is her story.

One wintry night in the north of Liverpool in 1932, a bowler-hatted man walked into Rose Hill Police Station. The desk sergeant, a Mr Davies, was enjoying a cup of tea at the time. The man, who was about 45, walked up to the counter and coolly stated: "I'd like to report a murder, sergeant." Sergeant Davies gulped his tea with a look of surprise and grabbed the log book.

"A murder?" he repeated, pencil at the ready.

"Yes, that's right," said the man in a matter-of-fact manner.

"Do you know the victim, sir?" he asked, without looking up.

"Yes, it's me!" came the reply.

The sergeant closed the log book and sighed. The station had more than its fair share of unbalanced characters making ludicrous statements.

"Really sir? Well you're looking quite well considering. Is there a full moon out there tonight?"

"Sergeant, I have just been killed, I am quite serious," answered the man sternly.

"Go on then," smirked the sergeant, who had resumed drinking his tea. "Who killed you?"

"A mechanic called Frank Draper – from Boundary Street. I paid him to fix my brakes but he botched the job. I've just crashed into a wall on Vauxhall Road. I'm dead because of him."

Sergeant Davies scrutinised the man more carefully; there was something decidedly creepy about him. He left the counter and enlisted the help of a young constable to escort the unstable individual out of the station. However, when the sergeant and constable arrived at the counter, there was no sign of the strange visitor.

About forty minutes later, Sergeant Davies was told by a policeman from the dock road beat that a car had crashed into a wall on Vauxhall Road. It appeared that the driver, who was from Scotland Road, had probably died instantly upon impact. Apparently he had been wearing a bowler hat, just like the sinister man who had visited the police station. Out of curiosity, Sergeant Davies visited Boundary Street, and he came across a sign over a garage that read 'Frank Draper, car mechanic'. Davies called into the garage and discovered that Mr Draper had indeed been paid to fix the brakes of the vehicle that had crashed on Vauxhall Road.

A policeman convinced Sergeant Davies, against his better judgment, to visit the morgue to view the victim of the Vauxhall Road crash. When the body was wheeled out, Davies recoiled in horror – there could be no mistake – it was definitely the man who had come into the police station to report his own death.

An inquiry into the fatal crash established that it had been caused by the vehicle's badly adjusted brakes ...

The Pendle Necromancer

When a man of the cloth tells you a strange story, it does make the tale sound more convincing. The following story was told to me early in 2001, by a vicar who has now retired in Liverpool. I have obviously had to change a few details to preserve his anonymity.

In the long hot summer of 1976, Jeff, a 35-year-old Liverpool man, finally ended his four years of being a curate when he was finally ordained. He took over as the vicar of a church near Pendle in Lancashire. Jeff settled in well with the people of his parish, and one young lady in particular soon caught his attention. Her name was Samantha, a beautiful woman of about twenty years of age with long black hair, and a rather anaemic looking face. The thing that really attracted the Reverend to Samantha was her eyes; they were hypnotic, and very seductive.

Delivering his sermon in the pulpit on his first Sunday in the parish, the young vicar started to stammer and lose his thread. The older members of the congregation tutted, because they realised that the reverend was continually glancing at Samantha, who was sitting on the front pew, wearing a very short skirt. Two elderly ladies started to give little coughs of discontent, and Jeff continued with his sermon, which was about upholding the Commandments. For some strange reason, Jeff could not remember all of the Commandments, despite being very familiar with them. He apologised and explained that it was because it was his first sermon, and he looked at his notes and struggled to continue. But suddenly, the two elderly women who had coughed deliberately moments earlier to express their displeasure at the proceedings, suddenly started to cough again – only this time they both seemed to be having an asthma attack. They rose to their feet in distress and started to turn red in the face. Two men ushered the women out into the fresh air, and they soon recovered.

That night, the vicar had the most realistic dream he had ever had. He dreamt that he was making passionate love to Samantha and as he woke up he felt as if the girl's lips were still pressing against his mouth. Jeff became infatuated with Samantha, but she seemed to have little interest in him.

Two months later, Samantha's aunt, an Irish woman, passed away, and Samantha had the body put in an open coffin at her home so that her relatives could visit to pay their respects. The vicar bought a floral tribute and decided that he would visit her and say that, although he had not known her aunt, he was sure she had been a lovely woman – just as a ploy to get acquainted with the lovely Samantha.

So Jeff went over to Samantha's home at about 7.30pm, clutching a big bouquet of flowers. As he walked up the dark path to the house, he got the shock of his life. By the faint light of the coal fire inside the house, Jeff could see Samantha – and she was completely naked.

Jeff was a man of the cloth, but he was also a man, and he could not resist such temptation. He walked up to the ground floor window with his heart pounding in his ears, and he peeped through the window panes. Through a gap in the curtains he could clearly see the curious sight. Samantha was prancing around in front of the fire like a woman possessed. Then he noticed the coffin behind her on a stand, and in this coffin was the body of Samantha's late aunt. The deceased woman had her arms crossed over her chest.

Jeff moved away from the window, a little bit afraid, yet he just could not keep his eyes off the naked young woman. In his mind he apologised to God, then cautiously peeped back through the window. There was another girl there now, and she was also naked. She was also dancing about as well and Jeff thought he could hear someone singing in the house.

Then he saw something that chilled him to the bone and sent him hurtling away from the house. The body in the coffin started to move. The arms slowly uncrossed as the girls continued their manic dance. The vicar dropped the expensive flowers and sped off into the night, all amorous thoughts banished from his mind.

The funeral took place later that week, but as the vicar was conducting the service, he wondered if Samantha's aunt was actually in the coffin. He now realised that she and the other woman must be part of a witches' coven. Jeff told his superiors about his experiences, but they refused to believe him. Some time later, he met and married another local woman, but for years he was haunted by the experience. He even found sinister effigies on his doorstep and received many poison pen letters until he finally moved to another parish, away from the area.

Mirage on the Mount

The following intriguing tale was related to me by two listeners to my regular slot on the *Billy Butler Show* on BBC Radio Merseyside.

In the late 1970s, a couple from Skelmersdale, Peter and Jean, saved enough money to go on a holiday to the Holy Land. Peter was an atheist, so he had argued that the money could have been better spent on a trip to America or Australia, but Jean said she wanted to go to Israel for personal reasons. Those personal reasons were that she was having a crisis of faith. She had also recently discovered a lump in her breast, and had feared the worst. She had not told anyone yet, not even Peter, and could not bring herself to visit the doctor.

Anyway, the Skelmersdale couple flew out to the Holy Land, and although the area was even then a dangerous hot spot, during their time there, Peter and Jean saw no trouble, just ordinary people getting on with their lives. They visited Jerusalem, and saw all the principal places where Jesus had been in his short life. They not only walked along the steps where he had dragged his cross on the way to the crucifixion, but were also whisked across the desert by helicopter to the place where Jesus had spent weeks fasting in the wilderness.

One day at the hotel, Peter looked up from his meal and noticed that Jean's eyes were brimming with tears, and he asked her what was troubling her. She became all choked up.

"I found, I found a – a lump in my breast, and I'm so scared," she blurted out.

Peter recoiled in shock.

"What, what do you mean, a lump? Have you been to the doctor's?"

The news devastated him.

When they were in bed later that night, Jean took his hand and placed it on her breast. Peter could feel a small, hard lump and his heart sank.

"You're going to the doctor's as soon as we get home," he said, trying to keep the panic out of his voice.

Jean started to shake slightly as she sobbed.

"Some holiday this has turned out to be," sighed Peter, which made Jean worse. He apologised and hugged her through the entire night. This was the last night of the holiday.

That morning Jean woke up and noticed that her husband was no longer beside her in bed. Then she heard a low whispering noise. When she slowly turned in the bed and glanced across the room, she saw Peter kneeling in front of an old cross on the wall. He was praying fervently, something she had never seen him do before.

"Please save my wife, Lord," he pleaded, over and over again. It was a deeply touching sight – Peter had been an atheist for as long as she had known him.

On that last day in the Holy Land, a tour guide escorted Peter and Jean and eleven other tourists around the Mount of Olives – nowadays called the Mount of Beatitudes. It was an unbearably hot and sunny day, and the mount seemed to shimmer with the intense heat. Suddenly, the guide called them all together: "Come along, this way quickly." A multitude of unsavoury looking people was approaching. They surged up the mount, towards the church at the top, and seemed to be excited as they were all chattering and chanting. This could only mean trouble, so the guide tried to usher the holidaymakers to a place of safety.

Then Jean noticed a curious sight; an old woman in black with a walking stick, was struggling to climb up the mount. The woman could hardly make it, so Jean decided to help her. Suddenly, the crowd thronged towards her and Peter and the guide, and only then did the guide realise that the people in the crowd were poverty stricken, for the clothes they wore were ragged and crude. Peter shouted to Jean, and then began to fret, because he was losing sight of her in the dust that the crowd was kicking up. It was like a stampede. The guide was a small but very strong muscular man, and he grabbed hold of Peter's arm and cried out over the din: "You'll be trampled to death, come over here". And he pulled Peter all the way down the hill. The guide then instructed the tourists to hurry back to their hotels and he scrambled back up the mount in search of Jean.

At this point, events took a mysterious turn. As the guide climbed up the mount, he could see the image of the crowd shimmering in the heat. Then all at once they started to fade away. However, the guide could still hear their voices, and they were speaking in an unknown tongue which he later learned to be Aramaic, which was the language that Jesus had spoken. The guide found only one person on the mount, and she seemed to be in a trance-like state. It was Jean. She said that she had been watching Jesus delivering the Sermon on the Mount, and she had understood every word. She related how, during the sermon, he had turned to her and asked: "What father would give his child a snake if he asked for bread, or a stone if he asked for fish? Ask God and he will give you good things. Seek and you will find. Knock and the door will be opened."

The guide looked anxiously around, and felt very uneasy; he could not get over the mass vanishing of all those people. He gradually came to accept that he had somehow witnessed a ghostly re-enactment of the Sermon on the Mount, and he brought Jean back down to her distraught husband.

Later that day, Jean discovered that the lump in her breast had completely vanished. It did not return and, to this day, she and Peter still pray to God.

Peeping Tom

The following strange story took place in the late 19th century in an area of Birkenhead bounded by Watson Street, Duke Street, Cleveland Street and North Conway Street.

One windy January night in 1885, Rosanna Cuff, a 20-year-old servant girl, was peeling potatoes in the kitchen of a house on Brook Street, when she felt a tingling sensation of uneasiness on the nape of her neck. Rosanna usually felt this sensation when she was being watched. She therefore turned, and gazed at the long windows of the kitchen, and through the top pane, she saw a full moon hanging in the sky, just visible between the curtains. The maid's gaze then turned to the lower panes, and there, between the small gap in the drapes, she saw what she later described as a pair of evil, smiling eyes. Rosanna let out a yelp, and ran headlong out of the kitchen to tell the master of the house, a Mr Edward Manney Jones, a man of almost 80 years of age.

Despite his age, Manney Jones, accompanied by his butler, immediately ran into the backyard. The butler brandished a poker, and Mr Manney Jones wielded an old sword, but the prowler was nowhere to be seen. However, more reports of the creepy peeping Tom came into the local police station.

A poor housewife at a house on Watson Street had been soaking in a tin bath at midnight in front of the dying embers of her kitchen fire, when she saw a face at her window. The lower half of the face was hidden behind a dark scarf, and the head was covered in a cap of some sort. The naked woman covered her breasts and threw the soap at the window before screaming for her husband. The sinister voyeur was also seen gazing lustfully through the basement window of a house on Price Street at two young maids who were playfully dancing with each other.

The police stepped up their patrols in the area, but the peeking pervert's escapades became even more audacious. At a lodging house near Duke Street, a buxom young lady awoke to find a letter on her bedside cabinet. The note read: 'I could have had you last night. I left my mark on your face.'

The young woman rushed to a mirror, and was horrified to see two black smear marks on each cheek. They seemed to have been made by soot being wiped onto her cheeks by someone's finger. The news of the daring intruder spread like wildfire, and within a fortnight, there were five reports of girls and women waking up to find soot-marks on their faces and breasts. Whether it was the mark of the prowler, or the work of pranksters, may never be known. One widowed woman screamed out in the dead of night and brought every member of her family rushing into her bedroom, but it had been a false alarm. The tail of the family cat had merely brushed against the woman's face as she slept. In the meantime, the hunt went on for the peeping Tom and everyone speculated on his true identity.

A local fishmonger, Peter Jones, became a suspect after a woman claimed that she had often caught him squinting through keyholes when he was younger. A butcher on Watson Street conjectured that the peeping Tom was a certain elderly policeman who had become sex-crazed after his wife had deserted him. A well-to-do businessman, Harold Gaines, of Park Road, offered a reward of £500 for information that would lead to the apprehension of the nocturnal snooper. Mr Gaines got the shock of his life when he awoke one morning to be told that his maid-of-all-work and cook, both women in their thirties, had found soot marks on their faces and undergarments: the calling card of the phantom-like peeping Tom. This time he had been clever enough to get past front and back doors that had been bolted at the top and bottom.

One stormy night a few weeks later, a habitual drunk named Alfie Randles walked home to his house on Park Road, in his usual befuddled state. He tried to get his key in the door, but kept missing the keyhole because he was so drunk. In the end, Alfie tried the doorknob instead, and to his surprise, the door opened. He staggered into the hallway, and noticed that a new gas mantle had been put up, and new flocked wallpaper now hung in the lobby. Alfie wondered where his wife had got the money from to decorate, so he went into the sitting room to ask her, but she was not there. The parlour looked entirely different to the drunken Mr Randles – then he slowly realised that he had walked into the wrong house. Not only that, he had also unwittingly stumbled upon the house of the mysterious peeping Tom. A man stood there in black clothing, the lower half of his face hidden behind a black silk scarf, whilst on his head he wore a river pilot's black leather cap, with the peak pulled down over his eyes. The man in black reached for the poker in the grate, then charged at Alfie Randles, whose legs were wobbly with terror. Randles ran into the hallway, almost wrenched the knob off the vestibule door, then threw himself to the front door. He opened the door and stumbled down the steps, whimpering.

The door behind him slammed shut, and the number upon that door was 54 – the number of Harold Gaines's house. The well-to-do top-hatted businessman was the peeping Tom. The police were alerted, and officers pounded on the door. The neighbours crowded around, and when Mr Gaines finally opened the door in his nightshirt, the police constables and a detective stormed the house. A full hour passed before the police left, and when they did so, Mr Gaines smiled at his doorway and bade the men of the law goodnight. There were rumours that he had bribed the policemen.

The peeping Tom reports suddenly ceased. But just under a year later, Harold Gaines died from complications of pneumonia, and days after his death, people reported seeing eyes gazing at them through windows – including a window that was on the second floor of a residence. Most believed the peeping Tom was the ghost of Harold Gaines, still snooping from beyond the grave!

Ghostly Piano

This is a very strange story that took place in a street off Upton Park Road, not far from Birkenhead Park, in the 1960s.

In 1966, a 22-year-old woman called Nancy moved into a terraced house in a certain street off Upton Park Road. Nancy was a very innocent girl, but she was quite sociable, and it was not long before she met a young man in the area. His name was Bobby, and he worked in a local factory. His weekly wage was pretty meagre, but he was a very proud and honest person who refused to take money off anyone, especially Nancy. When Nancy's beloved grandmother died, the old woman had left Nancy a small fortune, so Nancy did not need to work for a while. Bobby felt a bit intimidated by the situation, because he wanted to be the breadwinner. It was just a macho hang-up he had.

Before Nancy met Bobby, she had made friends with Audrey, a 30-year-old woman from a large family off Upton Park Road; she and Nancy got on really well. They had even been to a few clubs together, and Nancy had stayed over with Audrey's family a few times.

One Saturday night, Nancy and Bobby went to the Cavern Club in Liverpool, and while Nancy was dancing with Bobby, she noticed that he was not his normal, cheerful self. He seemed to have something playing on his mind. Nancy took him aside and asked him what was wrong, but was unable to hear his reply because of the thumping sound of the live band. Frustrated and annoyed because he was spoiling their whole evening, she ended up storming out on Bobby. He caught up with her at the Pier Head, where they ended up drinking coffee and discussing their future. Bobby said he had heard a strong rumour that the factory he had been working in might be closing in the near future, and he would have to find a better job. Until then, he would somehow have to find enough money to be able to take Nancy out and buy her things. Nancy told him not to be so stupid, because she loved him anyway. The couple then bought a bag of chips and went home to Birkenhead.

Nancy got back to find that her house had been burgled. Money she kept in a drawer had been taken, along with her TV, radio and a few other items. Bobby shook his head in despair, and then all of a sudden, Nancy ran into the back parlour. Her most prized possession had gone. It had been an antique Collard & Collard upright piano. It had belonged to Nancy's late grandmother, and was worth hundreds of pounds. From the scrape-marks on the floor, Nancy and Bobby could easily see that the thieves had taken the piano out of the back door. The alleyway was a short distance from a road where a van had probably been waiting to take the valuable piano away. There had been no forced entry, so a key must have been used. The police investigated and just said they would keep a look out for the piano at the shops of antique dealers and secondhand stores.

On the following day, Bobby did not turn up at Nancy's home. The girl sat in the parlour with her best friend Audrey in a depressed state. Then she received another shock. Audrey said, "Just between you and me, Nancy, I think Bobby had something to do with the break-in." Nancy was furious at the suggestion, and said that it was a ridiculous idea. Bobby loved her. Audrey pointed out that she knew hardly anything about Bobby's past and then she dropped a bombshell.

"Nancy, please don't repeat this, but did you know that Bobby knocks around with robbers?"

Nancy recoiled. "Bobby? Where did you hear that?" she demanded.

Audrey said she had seen him drinking with well-known house-breakers. "I think he probably gave your spare key to a friend and they had a copy made."

"No, not my Bobby. He loves me," Nancy insisted.

"Nancy, where is he tonight then? They say a guilty conscience needs no accuser. I bet he won't come near you again," predicted Audrey, with a total lack of tact.

Nancy suddenly burst into tears. It all made sense now. That was why Bobby had been preoccupied in the Cavern; he knew his friends were breaking into his girlfriend's house and must have felt guilty about it.

Audrey comforted her friend and brought her round to her own house, where the family tried to cheer her up. They sat her at the head of the table and Audrey's mother served her a fine meal. At eleven o'clock that night, Nancy and all Audrey's family heard the sounds of a piano; a piano playing a familiar melody; *No Place Like Home*. Nancy stood up and said: "That's my piano. That's the song my grandmother always played." Audrey's family looked at each other, mystified.

"Audrey, is my piano in this house? It is, isn't it?" said Nancy.

Audrey assured her that it certainly was not, and seemed hurt and stung by the accusation.

"Well where's that noise coming from then?" Nancy asked, exasperated, and marched out into the hallway.

From there it was obvious that the piano music was coming from next door, where a respectable elderly couple lived. Nancy hammered on the door, and an old man answered, with his elderly wife hovering behind him, looking bewildered. Nancy barged past them, followed by Audrey and two of her brothers. There, in the parlour, they found Nancy's antique piano, and it was playing *No Place Like Home* all by itself. As everyone looked on, the ghostly keys came to a halt.

The police later found out that the old man's son, who was the local window cleaner, had seen the piano in the back parlour of Nancy's home during his rounds, and had got a local crook to pick the lock of the back door. The window cleaner had then stored the stolen piano at his parents' home. Nancy also discovered that Audrey had been making approaches to Bobby behind her back. She had tried to get Nancy to finish with him by insinuating that he associated with crooks. Nancy asked Bobby if this had been the thing that had been bothering him and he admitted that it was, but then reassured her that she was the only girl for him. And the couple subsequently married.

To this day, Nancy believes that the ghost of her beloved grandma played that piano that night.

Gladstone's Atlantis Bill

At Number 62 Rodney Street, there is a plaque which reads: 'Gladstone, four times Prime Minister, born in this house, 29th December 1809'. Gladstone was an impressive reformer, legislator and legendary orator who dominated politics alongside his Conservative opponent, Disraeli. Gladstone was not an imaginative man, given to flights of fancy; he was a tough politician, who produced the Home Rule Bills and strove in the midst of controversy to bring peace to Ireland's troubles. Imagine then, how astonished and bemused the members of the House of Commons were in 1886, when Prime Minister Gladstone rose to his feet and attempted to get a bill through Parliament. Not some reform bill – but 'a bill to furnish funds to search for the legendary sunken continent of Atlantis'.

There were hoots and howls of derisive laughter from the benches on both sides of the House. Many decided that the 77-year-old Prime Minister must suddenly have become senile, and Gladstone's astonishing proposal was defeated. Many also wondered what had convinced the mundane and practical Gladstone to seek funds for such an outlandish expedition.

There were two reasons: in secret, Gladstone had read a book about Atlantis, an island that is said to have vanished below the Atlantic in the middle of the night, some 10,500 years before the birth of Christ. That book, by an American Congressman named Ignatius Donnelly, captured Gladstone's imagination. Gladstone had also recently heard about an incredible incident concerning a Lancashire adventurer called James T Morgan. About two years previously, Morgan had been returning to Liverpool from Brazil, where he had been exploring the Matto Grosso and the Amazon for gold.

When the ship was in the middle of the Atlantic, about 900 miles from the Azores, a lookout spotted a strange sight. A dark, triangular mass was visible in the sea, quite a few miles distant. By early evening the ship was within a mile of the mass and the Captain and crew could barely believe their eyes. The tip of an enormous black pyramid was projecting out of the water. The ship's compass started spinning wildly, as if the pyramid was magnetic. The Brazilian captain fully intended to sail straight past the strange object, but Morgan urged him to drop the anchor.

The captain grudgingly relented, and allowed Morgan and four of the crew to row a lifeboat over to the pyramid to take a brief look. The structure was made of basalt, and was estimated to have been twice as high as the Great Pyramid at Giza in Egypt. Morgan and the ship's navigator estimated that the pyramid was a staggering 960 feet in height. It had ledge-like steps going halfway up the structure, and Morgan attempted to climb the steps, but they were coated with slippery marine vegetation, which made them far too treacherous for him to proceed any further.

Morgan and the crewmen returned to the ship and made further measurements of the pyramid using the ship's instruments. The structure obviously continued downwards underwater for quite a distance, so estimating its true dimensions was impossible. During the night, a strange faint glow, like St Elmo's fire, gathered around the tip of the pyramid, and at three o'clock in the morning, the captain insisted that he must sail to Liverpool, in order to keep his deadline.

When other ships surveyed the same location near the Azores some months later, there was no sign of the mysterious dark pyramid. It was as if it had plunged back into the depths of the Atlantic from whence it came.

Was the pyramid the remains of some Atlantean temple that had been thrust up to the surface as a result of some volcanic upheaval, only to sink back into oblivion?

Romaine of Rodney Street

In the 1920s and 1930s, a very strange man named Alaric Romaine lived at 16 Rodney Street. At that time, in the front page columns of the *Liverpool Echo*, Romaine was advertised as, 'a private detective who gets results'. Romaine is something of a mystery, he was described as being of foreign appearance – some said he was Hungarian. What was unusual about him was his unorthodox methods of detection. He claimed that he could occasionally read minds. He also said that he had an ability to receive psychic impressions from objects found at the scene of a crime, which enabled him to piece together what had happened.

In January 1930, a woman named Clara Simmons called on Mr Romaine at his Rodney Street office. She brought him a small photograph of a handsome looking man with a pencil moustache and told him that it was her brother Robert. Clara recounted how she had had a petty argument with him a year ago and that he had not been in touch with her since. She asked Romaine if he could use his unique powers to find the man. Romaine then did a curious thing. He asked Clara if he could study her palm. The woman consented and offered him her hand. With his index finger, Romaine gently traced the fine lines on the woman's palm, and Clara seemed fascinated. However, this was actually Romaine's gimmick for reading a person's mind. He had learned this technique from the Indian fortune tellers during his days in

Delhi. The Indian fakirs distract a person by getting them to focus their attention on their hand, and when a person drops his guard in that way, it is supposedly possible to read their mind. Romaine suddenly dropped the woman's palm.

"Robert isn't your brother – he's your lover," he declared dramatically. "And you are a married woman." Clara Simmons gasped with shock but Romaine persisted. "You are carrying his baby and he has deserted you. You want me to find him of course."

Miss Simmons ended her charade and gave a little sob. Romaine felt pity for the woman and told her: "The father of your child lives on the south coast now. I see water. I'd say Bournemouth or Brighton."

Clara then confided that Robert's family was from Boscombe – a suburb of Bournemouth. Whether Clara ever caught up with her errant lover is unknown.

On another occasion, a Mr Ling, from Chinatown, visited Romaine and said that someone had been stealing from his home. Mr Ling could not go to the police because he kept large amounts of opium on his premises, and they had also been stolen. Romaine visited the scene of the crime and picked up a sort of psychic trail, like a bloodhound following its nose. The trail led to Mr Ling's brother-in-law. Mr Ling was furious, and called Romaine a charlatan, but Romaine told the Chinaman to check the cellar of his brother-in-law's house. And, sure enough, in the cellar's floor safe, Mr Ling found the stolen opium and other expensive items taken from his home.

In 1939, upon the outbreak of war, Romaine was summoned to Whitehall to help the fight against the Nazis in an amazing operation code-named 'Green Mirror'. Romaine and a group of skilled magicians and illusionists, including a gifted music hall conjuror, Jasper Maskelyne, hid tanks, armies, and even an entire harbour. If you write to the Public Records Office and ask to see copies of the files on Romaine or Maskelyne, the London bureaucrats will tell you that the Public Records Office files are not due to be released until 2021.

However, here are a few of the things Romaine and the magicians did for the war effort: he somehow created images of British warships in the English Channel and made Montgomery's 150,000 troops, with 1,000 guns and tanks, invisible to Rommel. However, Romaine and Maskelyne's greatest achievement was making an entire harbour vanish. This was Alexandria Harbour in Egypt. Maskelyne and Romaine simply had all the harbour lights turned off, and the magicians then recreated the same pattern of lights in the desert. Around these lights, Romaine had explosive charges planted. When the German bombers flew over Alexandria, they saw the harbour was further to the west than they had expected and re-calibrated their instruments. Then, as they started dropping bombs, Romaine set off the explosives around the lights, so that it looked as if both cargo and ships were going up in flames. The real harbour, a few miles to the East, survived the night raid.

These are just some of the things Romaine of Rodney Street was involved in, but in 2021, the world will finally discover the full truth about him.

Bring Back My Danny to Me

The following story was related to me by a reformed drug addict, and his counsellor and several other people have backed up the story. I have had to change a few names for obvious reasons.

In 1996, a 36-year-old man called Danny was at a nightclub in Birkenhead, when a friend pestered him to try cocaine. Danny resisted at first, because his so-called friends accused him of being a bore, but in the end, simply because of peer pressure, he snorted the dangerous powder. It was not long before Danny's friends were persuading him to try ecstasy tablets. Danny really could not understand all the fuss about drugs, because he felt that he was in control of them; just like having a cup of tea when you felt like one, he thought.

Then Danny's life started to fall apart. His girlfriend left him for another man. The firm Danny worked for went into liquidation and Danny ended up on state benefits. At around this time, his cocaine habit went out of control, and he started to steal to feed his addiction. However, through constant use, the cocaine seemed to have lost its effect, so Danny decided to try heroin to recover the buzz he had lost, and he descended into a personal hell. His life revolved around getting the next fix, and he became anti-social and paranoid. His parents were both dead, and the aunt he looked upon as his mother was in hospital, gravely ill from angina, so Danny had no one to turn to.

Sweating and shaking with cold turkey, Danny unwisely hurried round to his dealer with a knife and demanded heroin, promising to pay him soon. Not surprisingly, the dealer's lackeys soon caught up with him. The severe beating that they gave him left him within an inch of his life. They bundled his battered body into the boot of a car and dumped him in a derelict house in a run-down street in Birkenhead in the dead of night. Danny was left frozen and trembling and barely able to move because of his injuries. Like a wounded animal, he eventually crawled up into a ball in a corner of the filthy room and started to whimper.

Then Danny noticed something out of the corner of his eye. The old fire grate in the house was filled with rubble and all manner of filth, yet a golden light flickered there. All of a sudden, a wonderful aroma filled his nostrils; the smell of something cooking. Then the lopsided dusty lampshade on the ceiling grew brighter and brighter, revealing the contents of the strangely familiar room. An old sofa, two armchairs, a dining table, overlaid with an immaculate cloth, on which was a quaint, tall, narrow-necked milk bottle – or a 'sterry' bottle as Danny recalled. Butter on a little dish, a plate of bread, a bowl of sugar and a bottle of 'Cheerio' sauce were also on the table. These simple things reminded him of another place where love had once been. A broadsheet *Liverpool Echo* was draped over the arm of an armchair, and a comic called *The Sparky*. And the fire in the grate seemed to warm Danny's frozen soul.

Then he got the shock of his life, because in walked the woman he had idolised in his childhood, his grandmother. She had raised him after his parents had died within six months of one another. Danny's heart sighed and in disbelief he whispered, "Gran," unable to believe she was actually there. Hadn't she died years ago? He was confused. He remembered finding her dead in her armchair, and crying his eyes out as he had tried desperately to wake her up. His grandmother walked over to him carrying a bowl of steaming scouse.

"Come on, lad, come and get your tea," she beamed.

"Okay, Gran," Danny said, struggling to his feet. He sat in his old chair – the one his grandmother used to tell him he would break if he kept rocking it backwards. Danny devoured the delicious scouse which seemed to nourish his mind as well as his body. Then came the homemade apple pie and 'Bird's' custard. His grandmother suddenly leaned over the table, wet her fingers, and brushed his straggly fringe aside. She had always done that. She put the copy of the *Sparky* comic on the table.

"Wasn't sure if you'd read that one," she smiled.

"No, I haven't, Gran, thanks." He got up, walked round the table and held out his arms to his her. This was the only love that could never die, he thought, the love for your grandmother. She hugged him, and soon he was in tears. "I've missed you, Gran," he sobbed.

"Ahh, come on sulks, don't cry," she cooed. Then she suddenly said: "I have to go soon Danny."

"Oh no, Gran, don't," he pleaded.

"I came back to ask you a favour."

"What is it, Gran?" asked Danny, eager to do anything to keep her there. "You want me to go on an errand?"

"I want my little Danny back. Please be good for your Gran, son bun. Don't put needles in your arm, please," she pleaded.

Danny promised that he would beat his addiction. Then the room was suddenly in darkness. The fire had gone, the table, everything. Then he felt those fingers again, affectionately brushing his fringe. He stumbled out of that derelict house and realised it had once been his childhood home where his grandmother had reared him. Danny was admitted to hospital, and subsequently made a miraculous recovery, thanks to a patient drugs counsellor.

He is now drug free, has a steady job, and is renovating the house where the ghost of his grandmother came back from the grave to save the child she loved.

Seabed Ghosts

In 1929, a 50-year-old deep-sea diver, Albert Wilkinson, descended into the murky waters of the Irish Sea to investigate an uncharted shipwreck on the seabed. He had made countless dives on the many wrecks of the Irish Sea over the years, and was not a man who imagined things. His only interests were salvage money and the recovery of treasure trove.

On this occasion, Wilkinson was lowered down into the waters with a new and powerful electric lamp. He walked across the silt of the seabed towards the unidentified shipwreck of a two-masted 19th century sailing ship. The vessel was listing precariously, at an almost 45-degree-angle, towards its starboard side and the nameplate was too rusted to read. Wilkinson shone his powerful lamp into a gaping hole in the hull, and a gigantic eel bolted out and flitted away.

Wilkinson cautiously entered the ship, with his canvas bag ready to collect any artefacts from the sunken wreck. What he encountered in that ship was to give him nightmares for many years to come. Standing inside were several dark, hazy figures. At first he thought they were just the shapes and shadows of a jumble of seaweed. But then he perceived a woman in a shawl holding what looked like a baby in her arms. Standing behind her in a row were four or five male figures, but he could not make out their features. He distinctly saw the woman's face though. It looked pale blue, and her dark eyes blinked at him with a lifeless expression.

Albert Wilkinson had encountered octupii, swordfish and sharks during his career, but this terrifying sight from the world of the supernatural, chilled him to the bone. In a blind panic, he scrambled out of the wreckage, and saw to his horror that the ship had started tilting slowly towards its starboard side. He just managed to squeeze through the jagged edged hole in the hull in the nick of time. As he frantically tugged on the emergency line, a cloud of disturbed sand enveloped him as the ship fell on its side and crumbled on the seabed, causing the sand to billow round it and obliterate it from view. Moments later, the men in the ship on the surface slowly and steadily reeled Wilkinson to safety to avoid him succumbing to the bends.

Wilkinson refused to make a return dive on the mysterious ship, but later lowered a funeral wreath, weighted down with lead weights, on the wreckage. He was convinced that he had encountered the ghosts of some of the drowned passengers of the old sunken sailing ship.

Shiro Ninja

Up until the 1970s, there was a mysterious three-storey house which stood on the corner of Crown Street and Grinfield Street in the Edge Hill district of Liverpool. The windows of this house were always shuttered, even in summer, and the only person who really knew the occupants was a man who delivered the coal. He knew both the elderly oriental-looking man named Mr Kan, and his servant, Mr Tenshi.

One freezing January morning in the late 1920s, the coalman was delivering winter fuel via an alleyway that ran from Smithdown Lane, when he witnessed a brutal incident. A young, timid looking man, aged about sixteen or seventeen, was being beaten up by a gang of five or six ruffians. They had pushed the youth into the alleyway, where they robbed him of his shoes and the few pennies he had in his pockets. The teenager was left semi-conscious after the coalman intervened and the gang ran off. The criminals were members of the notorious Tierney gang, named after their leader, Jim Tierney. The gang also specialised in robbing railway goods off the trains in Crown Street.

Hearing the commotion, old Mr Kan came out of his backyard and helped the wounded teenager into his home. The coalman followed them and watched as Mr Kan, who was believed to be Japanese, administered herbal medicine to the youth, who said his name was Patrick Munn. He had been orphaned since he was twelve, and had had a rough time living hand-to-mouth ever since. He was underweight and badly under-nourished, and generally in a pretty poor state.

Mr Kan took pity on the poor wretch and resolved to take him under his wing, and every week or so the coalman would call at the house on Crown Street, and with each visit he would note how Patrick was changing for the better. The youth's physique improved steadily, and one day, the coalman was amused to see Mr Kan's servant shaving the young man's head. The months went by and Kan taught the youth how to defend himself with the ancient martial arts. He drank only water, and ate only rice, oatmeal, raw meat, or uncooked fish. The transformation was amazing.

During one visit, the coalman watched the elderly Mr Kan showing Patrick how to punch through a hard wooden board. Kan said, "Don't punch the board; punch at a point just beyond it," and he proceeded to smash his fist right through it. On another occasion, Kan tied a rope around Patrick's ankle, and threaded it over the wheel of a ceiling pulley in the washroom. When he pulled the rope, Patrick's leg rose until it was vertical. Eventually, the young man could raise his leg vertically without the aid of the rope. Mr Kan would laugh and call the boy 'Shiro Ninja' – which means 'white Ninja' in Japanese. He dropped the name Patrick and instead called him 'Mono', meaning one, which was to be his new name. Mono became very adept in the ancient Japanese arts of fighting.

He was an excellent student, according to Mr Kan, and the coalman would often watch, spellbound as he and Mono sparred in the large backyard. Despite his age, Kan's reflexes were like lightning. The two of them would sometimes sit in the yard meditating for hours. The coalman was once told that it was possible for a Ninja to tell the time of day by looking into the eye of a cat. At noon, the cat's iris is a perfectly vertical slit, and there were then seven gradual changes in the cat's eye that corresponded to the hours of the day as the sun moved across the sky.

One Sunday evening, in an alleyway off Mason Street, Mr Kan and his protégé were on their way to visit a friend, when the Tierney gang surrounded them. One of the gang produced a cosh and tapped his hand with it menacingly as he joked about Mr Kan's pigtail.

Now, in the police files, there is a fascinating record of the injuries suffered by the infamous gang members after the confrontation which ensued. Of the seven present, five of them between them sustained a fractured jaw, a broken arm, multiple shin fractures, concussion, and one attacker had his spleen ruptured and came within a hair's breadth of dying. One person was responsible for these injuries: he was Patrick Munn, also known as Mono. He cited provocation and self defence and was not charged. Mr Kan, being an upright and respectable citizen, backed up his apprentice's version of events.

Years later, Patrick Munn is said to have gone on a spiritual pilgrimage to Japan, and what became of him is a mystery. Mr Kan died in the late 1940s, and some members of the oriental community in the city believed he was a rogue Ninja who settled in the port of Liverpool after fleeing from Japan in the 1890s, because he murdered a man who violated his sister. There were rumours that Kan had been involved with the mysterious Ninja slaying of a man in Liverpool in the 1930s (see *Haunted Liverpool* 3).

Soap Sally

This story is about one of the strangest people in the history of Liverpool's folklore. Some called her 'Soap Sally', others knew her as 'Dirty Mary', or the 'Dog Lady', because she often gave bones from the butcher's to any dogs she came across, and the grateful animals would trail behind her in packs.

Soap Sally was rarely spotted during the daytime, but once twilight fell, she would invariably make her appearance. She was mostly seen around the Lime Street, London Road and Seymour Street areas, but there were also reported sightings of her as far afield as Wavertree, Kensington and Old Swan. Sally wore a silk headscarf around her head, tied tightly under her chin. She also wore a long, grubby-looking coat, baggy tights, and quaint, black, buckled shoes. She would carry a small basket that held soap, pegs, and other items she tried to sell. Her sinister reputation was primarily due to her very distinctive appearance. She was about six feet in height, and had a pointed chin and a prominent, aquiline nose. Her thick bushy eyebrows met in the middle, above her piercing dark eyes. She obviously never put the soap she sold to use on herself, because she was filthy and reeked of body odour. However, her face was always plastered in make up, and some thought Soap Sally was actually a man in drag.

In the late 1950s, a twelve-year-old girl from Bootle named Patricia Campbell decided to leave home because her parents were always arguing. She delved into her mother's purse, took some money to pay for the bus fare, and decided to travel to Liverpool, where her best friend, Susan Saunders, lived, somewhere off Cambridge Street.

Pat arrived at Lime Street and went in search of her friend, but was unable to find her. She asked everyone, but no one had heard of the girl. Little Pat began to panic and started to wander about aimlessly. She thought about returning home, but decided that her quarrelsome parents would be livid if she went back, and she dismissed the idea. It was getting dark, and Lime Street was not a suitable place to be for a young girl. Pat was gazing up at the statue of the naked man over Lewis's, when a cold clammy hand suddenly covered her eyes.

"Ooh, Don't look at that young Miss," said a strange voice.

Pat let out a little squeal of fear. When the foul-smelling hands were removed, she looked up to see a tall, thin woman stooping over her. It was Soap Sally, but she did not introduce herself. She grabbed the girl by the hand, and started walking with her towards Copperas Hill. Pat's mind was working overtime to find a way to escape from the old crone's clutches.

"There's a policeman!" she shouted, and pointed across the road.

Soap Sally looked over to where she was pointing, but there was no policeman in sight. Pat used the opportunity to break free and, without looking back, ran like the wind up Lime Street, until she had a 'stitch' in her side. Pat Campbell thought about the woman who had tried to grab her and whose pungent body odour still filled her nostrils, and she shuddered. Then an unusual sight soon took the runaway girl's mind off the scary encounter: a dazzling advertisement on a hoarding on the corner of London Road, which showed a girl on a swing advertising 'Full Swing Lemonade'. The girl's image was made up of dozens of lights .

As Pat stood mesmerised by the illuminated advert, Soap Sally caught up with her and struck again, and this time she grabbed the girl's arm. Pat could not break free. Sally pulled what looked like a knife out of her covered basket, and said: "You'll never see your mummy or daddy again if you make a sound". And she bared her yellow teeth at Pat, who felt as if her legs were starting to buckle. She started to cry.

As Sally turned to go up Lord Nelson Street, she stopped in her tracks. Coming towards her was a teddy boy named Jimmy Fleet, a real 'hard-knock' from the Bullring tenements. Jimmy took one look at Soap Sally, and how she had hold of little Pat, and in one movement, he produced a flick-knife and clicked it open. Sally swore at him and pushed Pat forwards. Jimmy beckoned for the crying girl to come forward, and he positioned himself in front of her. Sally took out a carving knife from her basket and brandished it at the youth for a moment, but then thought better of it and turned and fled in a disappointed rage. As she ran across the road, she moved like a man, and curiously, had prominent calf muscles like a man.

In an uncharacteristically chivalrous gesture, Jimmy, the young tearaway, took Pat to the police station, from where she was returned to her parents in Bootle. The police made enquiries, and then visited a certain house on Seymour Street which was said to be Soap Sally's home, but got no answer. When two policemen looked through the front window, all they could see was a Yorkshire terrier looking back at them from a basket. A forced entry was made, but the place was deserted; even the terrier in the basket was a stuffed animal. So too was a budgie they found. When they interviewed people in the neighbourhood, the police heard all sorts of stories, including claims that the soap which Sally sold contained fat from human bodies, but that was probably just a fabrication.

It is said that about a month after her terrifying encounter with Soap Sally, Pat Campbell woke up at half-past three in the morning. Something was tapping on her bedroom window. To her horror, when she went to look out, there on the pavement was Soap Sally throwing little stones up at her. Sally pointed a grubby finger at the petrified girl, then made a cut throat gesture with her finger across her neck. She cackled and then ran off silently. Perhaps Pat had merely had a nightmare, but to her it seemed all too real.

Some people say that Soap Sally's ghost still walks the streets of Liverpool.

The Boar's Head

On Christmas Eve, 1805, a stagecoach was due to leave Wavertree, Liverpool, for a four-day journey to London. It was supposed to have left Liverpool four days earlier, but heavy snowstorms had delayed its departure. Ten passengers had enjoyed their breakfast at The Lamb, an inn which catered for travellers in Wavertree. The time was six o'clock in the morning, and the ten people were seated at a large table, eating and drinking before departing on their arduous journey. John Ponsonby, an elderly and obese businessman, sat with his large back to the open fire, blocking off the warmth from all the others. Ponsonby had a voracious appetite, and he scoffed away, cramming mutton, roast potatoes and peas into his mouth as if this was his last meal on earth. He also had a disgusting habit of talking about his business intentions as he chewed enormous mouthsful of food.

One of the travellers had been taken ill, so there was a vacant seat in the crowded coach. Now, that same morning, the local rake, a young troublemaker named Robert Matty, was released from the lockup, a small local gaol which still stands today near Wavertree's Picton Clock. Matty had spent a night in the lockup for being drunk and disorderly. His aunt marched him up to Billy Rigg, the landlord of the Lamb, and paid the fare to have Matty taken to London, where his Uncle Jack worked. She hoped Matty would be employed by his uncle and begin to settle down at last.

Matty was allotted the vacant seat on the coach, and at half-past-six, the stagecoach was ready, and the ten travellers climbed aboard. The four poorer passengers sat outside on special roof seats, open to the elements. No sooner had the stagecoach trundled off down what is now Childwall Valley Road, than heavy snow started to fall once more. The four powerful horses galloped on as the coachman cracked this whip. When the stagecoach had passed Knutsford, later that day, a blizzard began to rage. The fat old businessman, Mr Ponsonby, swigged from his brandy flask, and the young lad Matty audaciously snatched it from him and took a swig himself. The coach started to slow down as the horses laboured through ever deeper snowdrifts The coachman called for people to help him shovel a path through the snow and ice, but the only man who left the coach to help him was a Lancashire preacher named Samuel Birchall. He shook his head in disgust at the selfish passengers.

"Many can help one, but one can't help many," he said pointedly, but his companions just ignored him and the four shivering passengers on the coach roof barged past him into the vehicle's slightly warmer interior. The preacher and the coachman battled against the worsening blizzard, shovelling furiously. If they could not clear a path, the coach would be snow-bound.

Young Matty leant out of the window and pointed at something in the distance. "Look, there's a light!" he cried. It looked like the grey outline of a cottage, with a stable next to it, just a short distance away. Lights were burning in the dwelling. The coachman decided to try and take the stagecoach over to the cottage, where the owner might allow him to shelter the horses in the stable until the weather improved.

When the coach arrived, the coachman and travellers saw that the cottage was in fact a large inn. The coachman wiped the snowflakes from the window and peered inside. People inside were eating, drinking and dancing, and a huge welcoming log fire was blazing in the grate. The coachman entered with Reverend Birchall and young Matty, and they approached the counter to talk to the innkeeper. They asked him if there was room for the travellers and themselves to stay at the inn. The jolly innkeeper's round, rosy face broke into a broad smile.

"Of course, bring them all in!" he said.

The travellers were soon seated with the other guests at a huge table. Greedy Mr Ponsonby drooled as a silver platter with a boar's head appeared. The boar's head had an apple in its mouth, and was surrounded by enormous roast potatoes covered with gravy and peas. Fine malt liquor, rum and stout was served, all on the house. The guests were overjoyed – they had been faced with the prospect of being marooned in the coach all night in the freezing blizzard – and now, here they were in the middle of a party! In the corner, a beautiful buxom woman sat on young Matty's knee and started to kiss him. The preacher sat by the fire watching the proceedings. The clock chimed midnight, and the preacher said: "Do you all realise that it is now Christmas?" Everyone went quiet. Taking a small Bible from his haversack, he began: "I will now read St Matthew's account of the birth of Jesus."

At that moment, the innkeeper started to snarl, and shouted: "No!"

Young Matty screamed, because the girl he had been kissing had somehow changed into an old hag. Then the boar's head on the plate opened its mouth, releasing the apple. Its beady eyes fixed on the preacher.

"Throw that book in the fire!" it ordered.

Meanwhile, old Mr Ponsonby had stopped gobbling down his meal and his face suddenly became contorted as he clutched his chest in agony. The shock of the talking boar's head had brought on a heart attack. Within seconds, his body crumpled, then clattered to the floor as he died, upon which the obscene boar's head roared with laughter. Dust fell from the oak beams of the inn and the ground shook. The log fire spat out sparks and flames, and most of the travellers made a sharp beeline for the door. Two of Mr Ponsonby's friends dragged his corpulent body from under the table, and a partly-chewed potato fell from the corpse's mouth. Another deep rumble stopped them in their tracks and they dropped Mr Ponsonby and careered through the door in terror.

The preacher remained, and realised that the inn was some cruel illusion created by the Devil. Matty screamed because the shrivelled-up harridan would not let go of him, but the preacher prised him loose from her bony fingers. The two men backed out of the inn and hurriedly stumbled through the snow drifts to the coach.

As the last passenger, Henry Long, was scrambling into the coach, he glanced back at the inn. A mound of gold coins had suddenly appeared in the hallway, and Henry, a desperately poor man, foolishly ran in to grab some of the glittering currency. But, as soon as he entered the inn, the heavy oaken doors slammed shut behind him, trapping him inside the devilish building. The entire inn was then swallowed up by the quaking ground, leaving the coachman and the remaining passengers huddled in the coach, shocked and dumbstruck. Turning their backs on the evil place, and the blizzard having now abated somewhat, they set off again on their journey, trying to make sense of the night's awful events as they were jostled and jolted by the coach as it lurched onwards over the rough, snow-covered roads.

When the coach finally arrived at Kidsgrove, near what is now Stoke-on-Trent, the travellers and coachman were still in a state of shock. All the people on the coach signed affidavits explaining how Mr Ponsonby had died from fright, and Henry Long had been engulfed by the diabolical inn as it sank into the ground.

And young Robert Matty never misbehaved again either!

Grey Ghost

In 1967, Paul, an 18-year-old Liverpool teenager, started dating Julie, a 16-year-old girl from the Claughton district of Wirral. She was very beautiful, and most of the boys at her school were madly in love with her, but Paul met her in the summer of 1967 during a school trip to Wales and started to see her. Julie was quite a demanding girl, and was used to getting her own way. She soon pestered Paul to get her an engagement ring and other items of jewellery to prove his love for her. Paul was only an apprentice painter, and he spent almost all his meagre wages on daily ferry fares to see his girl, as well as taking her out as often as he could.

Paul belonged to a notorious Toxteth family, well known to the police, and between June and August 1967, his three older brothers had allegedly broken into a number of tombs in St James's Cemetery. Most of the items stolen from the graves were items of Victorian and Edwardian jewellery, and somewhere along the line, Paul managed to obtain one of the purloined rings that had been wrenched from the bony fingers of one William Owen, who had died around 1860. This ring – a cygnet ring with a blood red stone – found its way onto the finger of Julie over in Claughton. It only fitted her middle finger, but she loved wearing it, and showing it off to all her friends.

In the September of 1967, a thick fog rolled over Merseyside one evening. Julie's father was alarmed to hear a frantic hammering of the knocker on his front door. He rushed out to find his teenaged daughter looking as if she was in shock; deathly pale and unable to talk. She had literally been struck dumb with terror. She fought to get past her father but he grabbed her wrists, and asked her what the matter was. Julie managed to gasp out just one word: "attacked". And she looked over her shoulder as if someone was following her.

Julie and her father then saw a figure emerging out of the fog. He wore a very tall top hat, and seemed to be grey from head to foot. Every part of him looked monochrome, as if he had stepped out of a black and white photograph. What really spooked Julie and her father was the way the figure moved through the low brick wall which surrounded the front garden. His legs appeared to pass straight through it.

Julie broke free of her father. She ran into the house, straight through the lounge, and out again via the back door.

Julie's father froze as he saw that the apparition had a black hook where his right hand should be and the ghost's face was terrifying. The eyes were as black as ebony and seemed to be boiling over with a terrible anger. Julie's father felt faint and then suffered a sharp pain in his chest. He staggered into the hallway and slammed the door shut behind him. Something started rapping on the door with an ominous, metallic sound. He was certain that it was the hook being tapped.

When he plucked up enough courage to peer through the curtains in the front room, he could see nothing at all, only the thick, swirling fog. Julie did not return that night, the terror-stricken girl stayed in her friend's house all night. When she eventually came home on the following sunny morning, she told her dad that the man in the top hat had followed her up Bidston Road in the fog. At first she thought it was just someone messing about, but then she noticed that the creepy figure made no sound as he walked and looked all grey, as if he were a photograph. She ran off to try and get away from him, but then he caught up with her and grabbed her hair. She managed to break free and kept running until she was exhausted and her side ached, and by then she had reached her front door. About a week later, the same figure was seen again by Julie's father as it stood at their garden gate. Moments later it seemed to evaporate into the air.

Around this time, one of Paul's ex-girlfriends bumped into Julie and told her that the ring she had been given had been stolen from a crypt. Julie confronted Paul and he betrayed his guilt by blushing bright red. She flung the ring at him and said that she never wanted to see him, or his stolen ring, again. From that time onwards, the ghostly man with the hook never bothered Julie or her family again.

In 1992 I was told that William Owen – the man whose grave had been robbed – had lost his hand in an accident and had had a hook fitted in its place.

The Little Folk of St James's Mount

In 1932, three children from the Bamber Bridge area went to stay with their aunt and uncle in Liverpool's Hope Street. The children were Susan Carmichael, aged thirteen, her younger brother David, aged eleven, and their little sister, six-year-old Lucy.

Uncle George was a great favourite with the children and one hot, sunny, June morning, he took the three excited youngsters to Liverpool Museum. Afterwards they watched the Punch and Judy Show in Lime

Street, before returning home to Hope Street for dinner. After that, Uncle George took Susan, David and Lucy to St James's Cemetery – which, as most Liverpool people know, is basically a gigantic quarry, about one hundred feet deep. As he read the paper and puffed on his pipe, the three children dashed off to explore the northern end of the cemetery, which has its own wooded area. It was here that something very strange took place. What happened there reached the ears of Canon Dwelly, the Vice Dean of Liverpool Cathedral. Susan and David were attempting to climb the steep hill in the shade of the trees when they heard a cry behind them. Lucy had fallen over and was lying face down in some ivy at the bottom of the hill.

"Go and pick her up, David," said Susan bossily, too absorbed in what she was doing to be bothered with her young sister.

"No, you pick her up, you're the eldest," said David, puffing and panting up the steep bank.

"You're the near ..." Susan turned around and her jaw dropped. She stopped in her tracks and David walked headfirst into her.

"What is it?" he asked.

"David, look!" Susan whispered, almost inaudibly, pointing backwards down the bank.

There, a tiny figure dressed in a brown, one-piece suit, was helping Lucy to her feet. His height was about three feet at most, but he was not a child, because his face looked too old. The strange figure gently brushed the soil off Lucy's dress and the little girl looked at him and smiled. She thought he looked funny.

"Oi, who are you?" called Susan from above.

"I'm Tarney," squeaked the peculiar little fellow, "and you're Lucy, you're David, and you're Susan," he added, correctly indicating each child in turn.

"Come here, Lucy, come along," shouted Susan, feeling decidedly uneasy.

David was also very nervous at the sight of the miniature figure. The man had a pointed chin and his eyes were a most unusual golden colour. So, plucking up all his courage, David scrambled back down the steep hill, towards his sister and the odd little man.

Tarney – as he called himself – suddenly waved his hand in the air and in his high-pitched voice shouted: "Bye for now". Then he ran with amazing speed and agility towards some moss covered rocks, and was soon lost from sight. The children ran at once to tell their Uncle George about the strange man, but he only half listened to their fantastic tale. "Get away with you!" he laughed, and continued reading his paper.

On the following morning, Susan was up very early when the doorbell rang. As none of the adults was up yet, she opened the door. A woman was standing there, reading a small piece of paper by the gate in Hope Street. She told a curious tale.

She said that a magpie had landed on the doorstep and had dropped a tiny envelope addressed to Susan.

"That's me!" cried Susan in delight.

The woman handed her the envelope, which she had already opened out of curiosity. A note inside said: 'Come down to play'. It was signed 'Tarney'.

The girl's heart skipped a beat. She showed the letter to her Auntie Mary, who thought the girl was joking, even though the envelope was tiny; a perfect miniature envelope. Susan or David obviously had not made it, it was far too skilfully made. Furthermore the message in it had been written in green ink – where would the children get hold of green ink?

Susan woke up David and Lucy and almost dragged them down to the cemetery that summer morning, and it was not long before strange things started to happen.

"I don't believe it. Look!" laughed David, and nodded towards the woods, where there were about five little figures, all dressed in brown like the little man who had helped Lucy to her feet – except that they were all wearing caps of some sort. They were throwing sods and stones at a group of figures which the children could hardly make out. These other figures looked rather frightening. They were smaller than the 'Brownies' as Susan called them. They were dark blue, and their heads were as round as a globe. They were throwing stones at the Brownies and laughing. One of the brown-clad figures turned around to face the children. It was Tarney.

"Throw stones at them!" he cried, gleefully.

The three children needed no encouragement and started to pelt the wiry figures in the woods with stones. The added onslaught soon made the little creatures flee into the woods.

Afterwards, the children were allegedly taken into a grotto of some sort, and Tarney explained that his people – he called them the 'Fay' – lived in a network of caverns running under the area of St James's Mount. They were always having battles with the 'Dwees' and the

'Ologs' – the round headed figures. The children were unquestioning, and delighted in this secret little world they had uncovered. They dreaded the day when they would have to return to their parents at Bamber Bridge. They began to regularly escape away to this magical miniature world, until one day Tarney said to Susan: "You won't see us again soon".

The girl became upset, and asked why.

"You'll come of age when the clock strikes thirteen," Tarney answered mysteriously.

Susan was puzzled at Tarney's words. But on the day before she was due to go back home, she invited the boy who lived next door round to play in her Aunt Mary's parlour. When Uncle George and Auntie Mary were in the backyard, the boy suddenly kissed Susan. It was her first ever kiss. At that moment, the old clock on the mantlepiece started to chime. It was noon, but for some mysterious reason, it chimed thirteen times. Susan immediately remembered Tarney's words. She rushed down to the wooded place, but saw and heard nothing. She never saw anything again, maybe because she had come of age. Perhaps the innocence of her childhood had come to an end.

The Vice Dean of the Cathedral heard the tale, and admitted that other people had reported seeing fairies down in those woods over the years. The usual explanations were put forward to dismiss the children's tales of the little folk. The flora down in St James's Cemetery was said to have hallucinogenic properties, which is a ridiculous claim, and even if the ferns and flowers in the cemetery could cause psychedelic visions, why did adults not see anything?

Strangely enough, St James's Mount was once the site of a mysterious village in Tudor times. Excavations carried out at the mount during the foundation-laying work for the Anglican cathedral in the early 20th century, revealed the statue of a woman. The statue had been placed at the centre of the village for some reason. It has been speculated that the statue depicted the legendary Liverpool witch, Ginny Greenteeth, who has always been associated with the mount. An early Liverpool song alludes to this connection: *On the Mount there is a lady, who she is I do not know.*

Perhaps there is some mystical correlation between St James's Mount, Ginny Greenteeth and the little folk that were allegedly encountered in St James's Cemetery by the three Carmichael children.

Storm in a Teacup

The following strange story took place in Liverpool in the early 1960s.

Around 1963 or 1964, Judy, a 20-year-old woman, was employed by a firm called Princes Pure Foods, which was located somewhere in the city centre. Judy worked in the cannery, canning such 'delicacies' as ox tongue, braised kidneys and pork luncheon meat. The mind-numbing job did not exactly pay well, but as Judy lived with her parents in the overcrowded family home on Peel Street, she did not have to spend much on domestic expenses, and always had enough cash to go out on the town with friends on a Friday and Saturday night.

One club she frequented was the world famous Cavern Club in Matthew Street, where the Beatles came to prominence, and this was the place where she met a very handsome-looking, 22-year-old man called Nicolas Lasarndt. He was tall and dark, and everyone remarked upon his striking resemblance to the French film heart-throb, Alain Delon. Nicolas had travelled to Liverpool just to be part of the Merseybeat scene, and was a so-called beat poet.

The Frenchman was staying at the YMCA, and one Saturday night after the Cavern was closing, he managed to smuggle Judy into his room. At their first meeting, Judy fell deeply in love with Nicolas, or Nick as she called him. He was a typically romantic Frenchman; reciting poems to her and buying her flowers and wine. Actually, the flowers had usually been stolen from Abercromby Park, and the wine was cheap plonk, but Judy thought Nick Lasarndt was the man she had dreamed about meeting for so long.

During her lunch hour one day, Nick visited Judy at work and announced, very publicly, that he had bought her a ring. All her workmates stopped what they were doing and watched with bated breath. Judy felt faint. Then Nick produced a novelty key-ring with a miniature flashlight as the fob. All the workers laughed, and Judy felt disappointed and humiliated. But then Nicolas smiled broadly and produced a small, velvet-lined box, and opened it. He got down on his bended knee. Judy threw her hands to her face in embarrassment as her workmates gasped. In French, Nicolas asked Judy if she would marry him. Tears dripped from the girl's eyes and she nodded, crying out, "Yes!" Upon which Nicolas kissed her knuckles and then slipped on the gold band. Everyone patted Judy and Nicolas on the back and gave a congratulatory cheer. Nicolas arranged for the wedding to be held in

Paris that June, at the church his family attended near Notre Dame. Judy could barely contain her excitement, and went on a shopping trip with her friends to find a wedding gown.

During the lunch break at the factory one day, an elderly woman named Mrs Magdalena was asked by one of the girls to read the tea leaves in her cup. The old lady had made some very accurate predictions in the past by studying the shapes made by the tea leaves at the bottom of a cup. The practice is known as 'Tasseomancy' in the occult world.

The elderly woman took hold of the cup which the girl had been drinking from, swirled the tea around three times, then turned it upside down over the old sink.

"Tap the cup!" she said to the girl, and she tapped the base of the upturned cup.

Mrs Magdalena righted the cup, and studied the shapes made by the soggy tea leaves for a while.

"Mm ... A man on a motorbike. Oh dear!" she sighed, frowning.

"What? What is it?" asked the girl apprehensively.

"Be very careful crossing the roads, dear," warned Mrs Magdalena. "That's all I can tell you."

A few days later, the girl came into work with a bandaged right hand. She showed it to the supervisor and asked if she could be let off work. The girl had been crossing Dale Street, and a motorcyclist sped past her, just missing her. The handlebar of the motorcycle grazed her, taking the skin off the back of her hand.

Everyone was stunned – including Judy, who thought the old woman obviously had special powers. She asked Mrs Magdalena to read her tea leaves. She was reluctant at first, but Judy insisted. A pot of Kardomah brand tea was brewed; Judy drank half of her cup, then Mrs Magdalena took hold of the cup, swirled the tea around three times, and turned it upside down over the old sink. Judy tapped the base of the cup. The pattern formed by the tea leaves was very odd. Clear for everyone to see, was the image of a man with a Van Dyke beard. There was a face close to his – a woman's face. What looked like hands were at her throat. There was also a small round face, a little girl's face in the cup.

"Oh dear!" Mrs Magdalena gasped. Another two women came over and saw the image as well. They asked Judy if she knew anyone with such a beard. She shook her head – she could not think of anyone. Mrs Magdalena swilled the cup quickly and went back to her work.

A fortnight before Judy was married, Nicolas returned from a three-week stay in Paris; to her surprise, he had grown a Van Dyke beard! This naturally gave Judy the creeps. Nicolas thought the beard added an air of authenticity to his beat poet image, but Judy inwardly shuddered. She said nothing about the bearded man glimpsed in the tea leaves.

A few days later, she was sitting in the YMCA lounge with Nicolas when in walked a young woman with long black hair. She marched over to Judy and Nicolas and spat at him. The globule of saliva landed squarely on his face and he wiped it away in disgust. The girl then started to shout unintelligible things at him in French. Seething with anger, he leapt up and grabbed her by the throat. He started to squeeze hard and shook her violently; until her eyes bulged in terror.

The girl passed out and Judy started to scream. Two men who had been playing chess in the lounge tackled the enraged Frenchman and managed to prise his hands away from the poor girl's throat. The throttling had left her throat red and bruised. The police arrived, and soon established that the victim was, in fact, Nicolas's wife of three years. It came to light that they had a little girl back home in Paris, who was ill. The frail child had repeatedly asked for her father, but he was too busy womanising in England.

Judy bitterly accepted that Nicolas was a complete cad and that if she had married him he would have become a bigamist. Trying to keep her self control, she flung the ring back at him, but as soon as she was out of his sight, she burst into tears and dejectedly made her way home.

All the dreadful events which had transpired that day, had been foreseen in the bottom of a teacup.

Two Terrifying Exorcisms

The following account was told to me by a Catholic priest who retired a few years ago. We were discussing the Rites of Exorcism, and he told me that even the holiest person is not immune to possession. True enough, it was recently claimed that Mother Theresa of Calcutta underwent exorcism shortly before her death.

The priest said that the Church frowned upon the undue sensationalism which the media creates when reporting exorcisms, and it was only after retirement that he could take the risk of relating a couple of his truly amazing tales to me, without bringing down the wrath of the Church upon his head.

I had never heard of this incident before, and after researching the claims of the priest, I believe it to be a true story. In 1956, Ray, a 13-year-old Liverpool schoolboy, went to town with his Uncle John. Ray collected stamps, so his uncle took him to McGoff's in Moorfields, a shop that specialised in stamps and philately. John bought Ray a pack of assorted stamps and they left the shop. As they were leaving, John bumped into a friend he had not seen in years. His name was George Terry. The two men started chatting, and suddenly, Ray tugged on his uncle's sleeve.

"What is it, Ray?" asked John, annoyed by his nephew's rude interruption.

"Uncle, that man's going to die tonight," he said, indicating George with his eyes.

This naturally caused something of a stir and Ray was reprimanded and told to remain quiet when adults were having a conversation. His uncle apologised to his friend George, but later that night, John was drinking in his local – a pub called the Swan Vaults on Conway Street in Everton – when he heard some shocking news. That very evening, his friend, George Terry, had finished eating his tea, had relaxed into his armchair, and had then died from natural causes. John thought about the morbid prediction his nephew had made earlier that day in Moorfields. John asked his nephew how he had known George would die.

"I get this smell – a sweet sickly smell," explained Ray. "I think it's the smell of some stuff they embalm bodies with, Uncle John."

On the following day, Ray's oldest sister, Janet, visited the family, bringing her little nine-month-old baby son with her. Ray asked if he could hold the baby, and Janet let him, but warned him to be very careful. Ray started rocking the baby in front of the fireplace, and suddenly, as the family was smiling and looking at him, the baby in his arms started babbling. Then it distinctly said: "Hello Janet," and started to cry.

Everyone recoiled with surprise.

"Did you hear that?" gasped Janet.

"I did that!" said Ray, upon which his sister snatched the baby back, and everyone felt very uneasy.

It had not been ventriloquism; the baby had spoken clearly in a low voice.

On the Monday morning, Ray's mother entered his bedroom to get him up for school, when she came upon a horrible sight. Ray was lying on his bed in his pyjamas, and a thick, gooey, brown liquid was oozing out of his mouth and his eyes. It smelt utterly vile. Ray's mother frantically called her sister to the room and they used towels to wipe away the foul liquid, but it kept welling up in Ray's mouth, eyes and then his ears. They tried to wake him up, fearful that he might choke, but he could not be roused. A doctor was called out, and he admitted that he was baffled by the brown, unidentifiable matter that had now swamped Ray and most of the bed.

Suddenly, the boy started to talk in a foreign language that the doctor recognised as Swahili. The doctor knew this because he had been raised in Kenya, where Swahili is spoken. Translating for the benefit of Ray's mother and aunt, he said that the schoolboy was muttering something about evil spirits. Ray's mother was alarmed by the state of her child, and the doctor suggested calling a priest. As the family was Catholic, they sent for their local priest, Father Elliot.

The priest duly turned up, and witnessed a remarkable and frightening sight: the boy, now covered in the filthy, brown, viscous liquid, started to levitate slowly off the bed as he screamed out in terror. Father Elliot, Ray's mother and aunt and a neighbour, frantically tried to pull the boy back down onto the bed, but they were all almost lifted off their feet by the unseen powerful force that was making Ray float. The boy rose to the ceiling, where he left a dark stain from the revolting material issuing from his mouth. The powerful force that was gripping him suddenly released him and he plunged back down onto the mattress. Then suddenly, in a raspy voice, unlike his own, Ray began to speak.

"We're taking the woman at Number forty-nine to Hell!" he rasped.

Living at Number 49 in Ray's street was a Mrs Katie Walsh, and that very night she died of a thrombosis in her sleep.

The priest decided to carry out the Rites of Exorcism on the boy using bell, book and candle, and he allegedly drove out five evil spirits, including the spirit of an Edwardian murderer. Ray returned to normality, and the priest visited him regularly for years, just to ensure that all was well. The boy was never possessed again.

The second exorcism which the elderly priest mentioned had been related to him by his uncle. Here are the unsettling events he disclosed:

In 1922, the father of a family of five living at a house on Livingston Drive contacted a Father Williams and told him that the dwelling was being haunted by a terrifying apparition. The priest was naturally sceptical at first, but he went along to the house in Aigburth and witnessed for himself the violent poltergeist activity. Knives flew out of a cutlery drawer and stabbed at the priest's palms, and on another occasion, hot lumps of glowing coal flew out of the fireplace, showering him and the family. An older priest soon arrived and advised the family to pack their bags and stay with relations until the 'problem' could be sorted out. They followed his advice without question and went to stay with relatives up in Spellow Lane, Kirkdale. They were all so distraught that the local parish priest had to counsel them.

The supernatural activity in the house on Livingston Drive became more intense. Yellowish acrid vapours rose from the carpets, and grotesque leering faces appeared on the walls in the form of damp stains. An investigator from a psychical research society fled from the house after seeing a demonic head appear in the flames of the fire. The head spat out something deeply personal, only understood by the man, which affected him so severely that he never returned to the house.

In the cellar of the abandoned house, the floor would at times seem to give way, and the cries of tormented voices could be heard. Holy water was thrown down there in copious amounts, but it only seemed to provoke the chilling sound of hysterical laughter. A neighbour who once dared to venture into the house to see what all the talk about ghosts was about, watched in horror as a huge, shiny, black beetle, about six inches long, came scrabbling after him down the hallway. He was so terrified that he flew out of the house in blind panic, and twisted his ankle on the front step.

Harry Price, a psychical researcher in London, also followed the case with interest when news of the inexplicable occurrences reached the capital.

An elderly nun who had dealt with visitations of the Devil, and was familiar with his crafty shenanigans, was asked to help. She left the convent in Hope Street and was driven to Livingston Drive. Clutched closely to her person, she carried her rosary, a Bible, and a silver crucifix. More importantly, she carried her faith, which was very strong. Probably much stronger than the average cleric's. As the car she was travelling in sped down Windsor Street, a swarm of hornets attacked the vehicle, and the driver had to veer off down Northumberland Street to escape the swarm. The nun suspected that the hornets were an obstacle from Satan to delay her. Then, as the old car was travelling up Park Road, the chassis started to shake violently, and the driver complained that something was wrong with the steering.

The nun ordered him to drive on and whispered a series of prayers; as she did so, the car gradually stopped vibrating. On Aigburth Road, a beautiful gleaming yellow Bentley screeched to a halt in front of their car. Two beautiful young ladies were in the Bentley, and the one who was driving sounded her horn and waved frantically at the driver of the nun's car. She was very attractive, and wore her hair in a stylish bob. The driver stopped the car and asked what the trouble was. He seemed entranced by the lady and her friend as they giggled and pointed to the bonnet of the Bentley. The nun left the vehicle and surveyed the ladies, who simply ignored her. The nun believed them to be another illusion of the Devil, conjured up to hinder and frustrate her attempts to reach the house on Livingston Drive. The nun urged the driver to take her to the house, but he seemed blissfully ignorant, because the two young ladies were taking off his jacket and telling him to fix the Bentley's engine.

The nun flagged down another vehicle and asked the driver to take her to Livingston Drive. He willingly agreed but, for some reason, he was unable to find the street. He had been reared in South Liverpool and knew the area well, but all of a sudden, he seemed confused, and he apologised to the nun. She left the car and found the house straightaway.

What happened next is not too clear, but years later, one of the priests recalled that the nun had gone down into the cellar reciting, "Though I walk through the valley of the shadow of death, I will fear no evil, for thou art with me," and so on.

About five minutes later, an enormous, long, shadowy entity – about 30 feet in length, rose out of the cellar and passed through the top of the house. It had two bright points of light on it which looked like eyes, and it faded away as it drifted over towards the local park, before vanishing into the evening sky. The nun allegedly claimed that the 'thing' had been one of the ancient fallen angels which had been cast down onto the earth with Lucifer a long time ago. She felt that it had been awakened by someone in the neighbourhood who had been dabbling with the occult.

Not long afterwards, the man who had helped the two ladies in the Bentley said that just after the nun had left, they had completely ignored him and had driven off without saying another word.

Voice in the Night

In June 1901, Stephen Donnelly, a young Cambridge undergraduate, was on vacation down in Devon at a small cottage in Exmouth. One night, at around twelve o'clock, he was reading a book in bed and gradually started to feel drowsy. He eventually turned the bedside oil lamp out and sank into a deep, dreamless sleep.

He was awakened some time later by the sound of a voice somewhere nearby. The bedroom was pitch black because the heavy drapes had been tightly drawn. Donnelly froze as he heard a voice which sounded very close saying: "Go down to the ferry".

The student slowly reached out for the bedside clock, ready to throw it at the intruder in his bedroom.

Then the voice said: "Go down to the ferry, the boatman awaits."

Donnelly bolted out of bed and ran to the window. He almost ripped down the curtains as he flung them apart. Moonlight flooded the empty room. Not a soul was to be seen.

Donnelly lit the oil lamp and thought about the strange voice. He wondered if he had been dreaming, and sat uneasily on the bed. After a while he tried to sleep again, only this time he felt more comfortable leaving the lamp lit. He exhaled in relief, adjusted his pillow, and closed his eyes. Moments later, the disembodied voice spoke again.

"Go down to the ferry, the boatman awaits," it said, this time more urgently.

Donnelly snapped open his eyes and quickly sat up in one reflexive movement. He looked about; there was still nobody there. Goosebumps erupted all over his skin.

"Who are you?" he asked, feeling slightly more curious than frightened.

There was no reply. The undergraduate got fully dressed, and as he was unable to sleep, decided to go for a walk down to the River Exe, which was not that far away. When he got to the ferry's small landing stage, he saw the dark hulking shape of a boat, barely visible through the thick mist hanging over the river. Suddenly, a loud voice boomed out: "Are you Donnelly?"

Out of the swirling mist on the pier walked a man with a grey beard. It was the ferryman, Mr Thorne, who lived across the River Exe at a place on the riverfront called Starcross.

Donnelly was puzzled. Mr Thorne then said that he had been roused from his sleep by a frantic voice outside his hut which had cried, "Mr Donnelly is waiting to be taken from across the river. A man's life depends on this!"

When Mr Thorne got outside he saw only the ghostly night vapours, tracing the contours of the riverbank. He assumed that someone on a passing boat had shouted the strange message, but he heard it again shortly afterwards, so he came across the river to see if a Mr Donnelly was waiting.

Donnelly instinctively boarded the ferry and told old Mr Thorne about the voice summoning him there. At the Starcross pier, Mr Thorne said he intended to get some sleep for an early rise the next morning and bid him goodnight. Stephen Donnelly ended up walking through the night, now separated from his home by the river.

At around 2am, the voice spoke again out of the night air, only this time it sounded even more forceful.

"Go north, to Exeter," it commanded.

That meant walking some five miles, but Donnelly was fascinated by the supernatural disembodied voice. He walked on, until the early summer dawn paled the sky. He eventually came to a hotel, and decided to have breakfast there. The place was unusually busy, as the assizes were being held at the nearby court. Donnelly learned that a carpenter, originally from Liverpool, had been arraigned on a capital charge, and was expected to be sentenced to hang, so people had come from miles around to crowd into the gallery at the court. On a whim, Donnelly also decided to go to the court.

The carpenter, a man named Jim Ashton, had been accused of killing a woman; all the evidence was circumstantial, but conviction seemed inevitable. If Mr Ashton could find only one witness to put him somewhere else at the time of the murder, he would escape the hangman's noose. But there was not even an opening for a defence, and the judge had the black cap at the ready.

All of a sudden, Stephen Donnelly, the man who had been lured to Exeter by a phantom voice, recognised the prisoner. He recalled that on the date of the murder, Jim Ashton had been the carpenter who had mended the sash-line of the cottage window at Exmouth. Donnelly told the court this, and the judge asked if he had any proof that the prisoner had been there. Donnelly thought hard – there must be something.

"Yes! wait a moment ..." he cried jubilantly, pulling a small brown object from his pocket. "This is the carpenter's pencil I borrowed from

Mr Ashton, to sign the invoice for the mended window. I forgot to give it him back and it ended up in my pocket."

Mr Donnelly also remembered that he had a copy of the invoice back at the cottage. When the new evidence was confirmed to be true, the jury returned a verdict of acquittal and Jim Ashton was released.

Donnelly told him the story about the phantom voice, and the Liverpool carpenter said, "Aye, I believe you. You heard my guardian angel". Ashton explained that something benevolent had been looking after him since he became an orphan in Liverpool many years ago. Mr Donnelly, and Mr Thorne the ferryman, signed an affidavit confirming that they had both heard the strange voice which saved a man from the gallows.

Warning at the Altar

In the year 1879, a fairly wealthy businessman called John Pickavance met a 20-year-old woman at a ball in Knotty Ash. Martha was a servant employed by the Warbrick family, and, as a special treat, she had been given the night off to attend the ball with the Warbricks' youngest daughter, Emily Warbrick, who was just sixteen.

John Pickavance, who was about 45 years old, and originally from Salford, approached Martha Brewster, who was said to have been exceptionally beautiful and to have possessed a lovely personality. Pickavance was balding, rather stout, and yet had a certain way with the opposite sex. He took hold of Martha's hand, kissed her knuckle, and asked the shy servant girl if she would care to dance with him. Martha accepted, and young Emily Warbrick watched the couple waltz away.

Mr Pickavance could not resist constantly embracing Martha and in the end, Emily had to literally pull the servant out of his lustful arms. Back at the Warbricks' house, Martha seemed to be in a dream, and she told Emily and her older sisters that she had agreed to see John Pickavance in a fortnight's time, on her next night off. However, on the following morning, Pickavance called at the Warbricks' house, and Martha answered the door in her servant's uniform. John Pickavance thrust a bouquet of scarlet roses at her, then got down on his knees. He kissed her hand and proclaimed his love for her. Martha blushed scarlet, and Mrs Warbrick and her three daughters came down to see what all the fuss was about. They were astonished to see Mr Pickavance with his arms around the servant's skirts, crying like a baby, and declaring that he had not experienced such an intense love since he was a schoolboy.

Anyway, Pickavance, being rather overweight and out of shape, had difficulty getting to his feet, and the Warbrick girls had to help him up. When he left, Martha wandered about in a dreamy daze. Mrs Warbrick was outraged at the unseemly carryings on, but the Warbrick girls took Martha into the kitchen and poured her a glass of claret in celebration. They were delighted by the romance, and excitedly predicted that it would not be long before wedding bells were ringing.

A fortnight later, Martha met her passionate admirer at another ball, and on this night, John Pickavance was anxiously scrutinising the dance floor. He complained that he had lost a silver locket which was of sentimental value, but the floor was so busy and poorly illuminated he was unable to find it. By pure chance, Martha found the tiny locket, and instead of immediately handing it to Pickavance, she went to powder her nose – with irrestistable curiosity she opened the locket. Inside was a miniature painted portrait of a woman – and the woman was the exact double of herself. Martha stared at it long and hard. After a time she composed herself and went back into the dance hall and pretended to find the locket, upon which John Pickavance snatched it from her. Martha asked him what was in it.

"Nothing, my dear," Pickavance answered, elusively.

Martha courted John Pickavance for almost six months, and the relationship naturally progressed to the stage where Pickavance proposed. Martha accepted, and the marriage was due to take place at St John the Evangelist's Church in Knotty Ash. However, John Pickavance had held a wild stag party the night before, and was so sick on the following morning, that he was half an hour late.

Martha waited and waited, becoming more and more fretful with each minute that passed, surrounded by anxious friends and relatives. The young maid started to cry, and her aunt tried to comfort her, "There! There! Don't you fret, he'll be ..." She stopped mid-sentence as she suddenly noticed the colour draining from Martha's face.

A thin woman, wearing a white hood, stepped forward from the crowd and approached Martha. It seemed that no one else could see her, but Martha almost fainted in shock, because the woman was wearing a burial shroud. And what is more, she had dark circles around her sunken eyes. The woman smiled at Martha, and the maid watched in horror as she pulled the shroud away from her neck to reveal a gaping slit. The woman's neck had been cut.

"He killed me! Wed him not," she whispered.

Martha Brewster screamed and ran out of that church. She passed a bewildered John Pickavance as he was climbing out of a hansom cab. Nobody else saw the ghost in the church, but when the jilted John Pickavance heard the strange tale, he withdrew all his money from his bank and immediately left Liverpool. We know that Mrs Matilda Pickavance had gone missing from her home in Manchester ten years before, and her body was never found. Had John Pickavance murdered her, and had her spirit returned from the grave to warn Martha Brewster?

The Werewolves of County Fermanagh

Werewolves are usually imagined to be people who have turned into wolves through some supernatural physiological process, but the origins of the werewolf tale hint that the creatures of the night are actually permanent wolf-like animals. The myth suggests that the people they bite do transform into humanoid versions of wolves (and not always when the moon is full) for a defined period of time, before reverting back to their original selves. Surely there is no hard evidence for such metamorphoses?

Well, there is a surprising number of testimonies from prominent and honest people, that reach from ancient times to the present day. For example, in the 15th century, Pierre Mamor, the Rector of a French university, wrote extensively on the werewolf from contemporary sightings and encounters. He relates the disturbing, well-witnessed account of a Lorraine peasant who watched in horrified disbelief as her farmer husband clutched his throat as he sat at the table, ready to eat. He started to vomit, and slowly, a small child's arm emerged from his mouth. Witnesses said the farmer had turned into a wolf the night before and had devoured a child. A priest later exorcised the farmer, and claimed that werewolves were demonic entities that could possess people and turn them into blood-hungry beasts. History abounds with such reports of the werewolf ranging from the terrifying Beast of Gevaudan, an unknown species of wolf that killed men, women in children in 18th century France, to the so-called mysterious 'big cats' of England, such as the Beast of Bodmin and the Surrey Puma.

The following strange story is from three separate sources: a Liverpool soldier who served in Northern Ireland in the 1970s, an old book on Irish folklore, and a few clippings from the Irish press.

The land along the border of County Fermanagh in Northern Ireland, is lonely and wild; consisting mostly of mountain, lake and bog, dotted here and there with small villages and hamlets tucked away around the bend of a road – Belcoo, Garrison and Derrygonnelly. In Fermanagh, the mist rolls back and forth across a bleak but beautiful landscape, lingering in the hollows and making weird shapes out of ancient standing stones. The region is famous for its caves and potholes, and there are many deep and still unfathomed caverns. For hundreds of years, people have heard strange beasts in these caverns. From time to time, people claim to have been lost in such places and it is a common belief that they have been 'carried away' to the dark realms below by the so-called werewolves of Fermanagh.

In 1978, a unit of nine soldiers (including one from Liverpool) were on a reconnaissance patrol in this part of County Fermanagh. At three o'clock in the morning, they camped in a wooded area overlooking a farm. Above the soldiers, a full moon shone down. The soldiers cursed such nights, when the moonlight showed them up. At precisely 3.15am, they were startled to hear what sounded like a diabolical choir of wolves – the howls coming from the direction of the mountains. The commander of the army unit dismissed the howls as people messing about; possibly late night revellers.

But whoever the howlers were – they were getting closer, and soon the soldiers saw four dark shapes materialise on a hillside, silhouetted against the full moon. They looked like wolves, only twice as big. The commander reasoned that the animals only looked bigger because they were on the horizon, but one of his men had a look at the creatures through infra red binoculars, and saw that these animals were enormous – he estimated their size as about seven feet in length. The unidentified creatures seemed to work as a pack, and they slowly surrounded a bull in the corner of a field. Cows and bulls sleep standing up and are pretty insensible when they are asleep. The unit watched in fascination as the animals simultaneously attacked the sleeping bull, and the sounds of its squeals and the loud snarls and roars of the wolflike animals had the soldiers nervously reaching for their SLR assault rifles. Three of the huge creatures escaped, each dragging a leg of the black Irish bull, which was left barely alive.

The soldiers watched in total amazement as the torso of Irish black heifer, which weighed about a thousand pounds, was hauled up the hillside by one of the mysterious predators. This creature looked silvery grey in the moonlight, whereas the other three were jet black. At one point, the creature suddenly tore out the throat of the bull, probably not to put it out of its misery, but because the dying Irish black bull was easier to drag in a lifeless state.

As soon as the four animals retreated silently over the hilltop, the commander set off for the spot where the attack had taken place, accompanied by three soldiers. They found a solitary leg and part of the hind quarters of the bull. The nerves in the leg were still twitching. They noted the huge clawmarks in the flesh and the trail of blood. All of a sudden, the large, grey, wolf-like animal made a reappearance. It pounded down the hill towards the four soldiers, snarling ferociously, with the bull's blood smeared around its jaws. The commander gave orders to fire, and two of the soldiers aimed their SLR rifles at the beast and opened fire. In two seconds, 80 rounds hit the animal, its body contorted and leapt high into the air as the bullets ripped through him. Then it rolled down the hillside, yelping, until the body juddered to a halt about 25 feet away from the soldiers. It looked like a wolf, but it was over seven feet in length, with a long body, and very long, muscular, hind legs. Its incisor fangs were six inches long.

The soldiers retreated as more of the creatures streamed down the hillside. They circled the body of their fallen comrade. Watching cautiously, the commander of the group told his men not to fire, as their weapons had already blown the reconnaissance patrol's cover. The creatures proceeded to drag the body of the overgrown wolf up the hillside.

At first light, the soldiers followed the trail of blood and discovered that it led into a vast system of mountain caves.

A week later, a group of Canadian wildlife experts investigated the sightings and tracks left by the animals and confirmed that a species of unknown creature was at large in the area.

In 1983, two soldiers were allegedly attacked by a creature in County Fermanagh. One of them showed the tear marks which the animal had made in his flak jacket with its claws. Both soldiers described the dangerous creature as a very large wolf, which ran off, seemingly wounded.

First Love – Last Love

Since 1990, I have been getting a few regular reports from people asking me if I have heard of the ghost of a rather forlorn-looking man who has been spotted at dusk – often in the autumnal months – standing near to the spot where the Blue Ball pub once stood. The Blue Ball was the place to be when the Fifties and Sixties were unfolding, and many famous rock and rollers, soul artists and Merseybeat groups performed there.

During my interviews with people regarding this pub, and the fabulous, feelgood, Merseybeat era, I was able to piece together the following touching story of a childhood romance. Some say that the only love that lasts forever is unrequited love, but I also believe that your first love never really dies.

At 9.30am on Thursday 4 October 1962, five schoolboys had been lined up to be given the cane by a teacher at a certain school near Kensington. The five boys knew perfectly well who had put a bucket of water on top of a door that had been left ajar in the classroom – but none of them was prepared to snitch on the culprit. The last lad in line was a thirteen-year-old named Billy McMahn. He had tragically lost his father the year before, and some thought that since then, the boy's behaviour had become uncontrollable.

As Billy heard the first whack of the cane hit the palm of the first boy in the line, he decided to escape and sneak out of school. He silently slipped away, wrapping his scarf over the bottom half of his face, imagining himself to be an outlaw of the wild west – on the run from the law, with a posse after him. He soon became bored, wandering through the morning streets, and was sauntering aimlessly down Prescot Street when he noticed a girl under a tree, collecting conkers. She was a pretty girl with a bob of black hair, a round baby face and big green eyes. She wore a large coat which partly covered her school uniform. Billy was immediately captivated by her.

"Hiya," he said.

"Hello. I'm collecting conkers," replied the girl, with a lovely Irish lilt to her voice.

"My name's Billy by the way," he continued, waiting for the girl to reveal her name. But she just carried on picking up the conkers on the pavement without saying a word.

"Hey! are you sagging? You should be at school shouldn't you?" said Billy, persevering.

Picking at a conker shell, the girl smiled wanly and shrugged her shoulders.

"I have to start at a school back in Ireland," she moaned. "I don't want to go because my friends are all here. I'm not going."

"Don't be soft, girl, you can't sag off school forever. I sagged off for a week once," smirked Billy, "but someone snitched."

"My name's Claire," she said, ignoring his comments. "Have you ever smoked?"

"Yeah! Cigars and pipes even."

"What's it like?" Claire asked, with an engrossed stare.

"Ciggies taste like liquorice," lied Billy, "I've packed them in now. I'm going in the Air Force you see. My Uncle's got a plane and he gives me lessons. I'll be getting a licence after I pass my test."

Claire was impressed.

"Well, Billy, can I ride in your plane when you get a licence?" she flirted.

Billy went all warm when the sweet girl said his name. This was the first time he had felt real love. Of course, he had had a crush on Connie Francis and an actress on the telly who played a nurse in *Emergency Ward 10*, but this was the first crush he had had on a real person. He delved into his pockets and produced a sticky bag of mintballs.

"Have one, er – Claire," he offered shyly.

The girl blushed and eventually managed to tear the sweet free of the paper bag.

It was not long before Billy was holding hands with Claire as he walked along in what seemed like a dream. She liked the same comics as him, the same films, even the same music.

"Hey, do you know this song?" asked Billy, and he started to sing a song called *Forget Me Not* by Eden Kane. Claire knew all the words, and said it was her favourite. It was as if they had been made for each other. The day of a child is much longer than an adult day, as it is packed with more concentrated activity, and time is in abundance. By the time evening was falling, Billy and Claire were at the Pier Head, where Billy had spent his entire pocket money on chicken soup for Claire because she was hungry. Claire and Billy looked up at the eternal stars, and she mused: "I wonder if there's another Billy out there on some planet?"

Billy gazed at the stars and squeezed her hand.

"Yeah, and say there's another Claire on some other planet millions of miles away and Billy never gets to meet her. I'd die if I could only see you through a telescope and never meet you."

And they suddenly embraced and kissed. Their first ever kiss, on the landing stage, 4 October 1962.

"I love you Claire," announced Billy.

"And I love you as well," Claire said, smiling back at him.

As they walked up Water Street, Claire pointed to a ledge on one of the old buildings.

"Ah, Billy, look!" she said.

"What?" he asked.

He could only see two pigeons with their heads nodding under their wings.

"Pigeons mate for life and remain faithful," Claire informed him. "So when you see three, that's a couple and a pigeon that's lost it's wife or husband. Ah!" she sighed.

Billy kissed Claire again.

"If we were pigeons," he said, "I'd stay away from kids with catapults and make sure you did as well."

The two young teenagers then spotted a policeman and they sloped off like thieves in the night.

While wearily walking across the expanse of Derby Square, Billy explained that his drunken uncle always drank in the Blue Ball pub on Prescot Street. He suggested that if they went there, he could think up a story which would allow Claire to stay awhile. His drunken Uncle Brian would not know any better. In fact, he would be lucky if he knew what day it was. Billy was sure he would let them both stay at his place. Billy said he could start a steady job on a good paper round and get a Saturday job as well. With these dreamy childish hopes in his mind, he confidently walked into the pub to find his inebriated uncle. But things did not go according to plan.

Uncle Brian had long been barred from the Blue Ball, and Billy was chased out of the pub. Moments later, a policeman from the bridewell next door to the Blue Ball grabbed him and Claire by their arms.

"Where are your parents?" he demanded.

Billy was trying to explain when Claire cried out: "There's my mum and dad!"

Her angry parents were marching up Moss Street. This was the end.

"Billy I love you," said Claire and went to kiss him but the policeman forced them apart.

"Claire, listen, please listen," said Billy urgently. "When we're sixteen we can get married."

Claire started to cry but the policeman just started laughing. "A right little Romeo aren't you?" he said.

"Meet me here three years from now. Three years to the day. I swear I'll wait for you. I swear," Billy cried.

Claire's parents grabbed her and started shouting. The policeman was talking in raised tones as well, as he shook Billy's arm, but the two teenagers heard nothing. They gazed at one another, two souls united, about to be separated forever.

"October the fourth – I'll be here Billy," sniffed Claire.

"So will I, Claire," Billy shouted, as he watched her parents drag her off down Moss Street to her home in Erskine Street. His first love was being taken away, worse still to Ireland. Billy struggled against the policeman's mighty arms and kept turning round to glance at his girl. Claire was also glancing back; a pale sorrowful face yearning to be with the boy she loved. She turned the corner and was gone.

For three years, throughout that hormonal cauldron known as adolescence, Billy loyally rejected the advances of every girl he met. He could not foresake Claire, and on 4 October 1965, he went to a café near the Blue Ball pub. He lingered in a window seat there early in the morning and waited for hours. He wondered if he had been a fool. Doubts crept into his mind as time dragged on, and he began to lose faith in his devotion for the Irish girl and battled to cling on to it. Maybe Claire was even dating someone else by now, he tortured himself.

Then at 12.30pm, he noticed a girl with black hair. She had a look of Claire, but seemed different. It was her older sister Patricia.

She had been visiting her Aunt Sissy in Erskine Street and had come to the spot outside the Blue Ball to deliver a letter to Billy on 4 October – just as Claire had repeatedly told her to. Tragically, the year before, at Christmas, Claire had died, at only fifteen, from leukaemia.

Billy read the letter Claire had written to him, apologising for not making the appointment, and sobbed without control. Claire's sister tried to comfort him, but Billy was inconsolable and wandered off, to the old chestnut tree where he had first set eyes on his love. Billy visited Claire's grave many times in Ireland and, in fact, never married. He died young in 1990. They say that around 4 October, you may see his ghost on Prescot Street, waiting for a girl who will never arrive.

Where's Alice?

My research is featured on a number of Internet websites, so I get a regular stream of emails from people all over the world who tell me they enjoy my stories, and often send me accounts of their own strange experiences. The following tale is from a man named Ryan who was born in Liverpool in 1979. When he was two, his family decided to emigrate to Allentown, Pennsylvania, and Ryan now lives in Orange County, California. The story begins in 1995.

Ryan was something of a loner. The 16-year-old Pennsylvanian had a small number of friends at his high school, but outside the school gates, he was a deeply lonely fellow. His parents and two older sisters were always urging him to unplug his PC and to get out and play sports like other teenagers. But Ryan was not interested in sport. He liked tossing a basketball into his slamdunk in the yard now and then, but he was more of a thinker. He read a lot, and was especially keen on books by Ray Bradbury.

But he had another avid interest, and that was a girl who lived down the street named Bethany; a shapely girl with long, straight, strawberry-blonde hair, a peaches and cream complexion, and a pair of smouldering brown eyes which set many male hearts in the neighbourhood alight. Bethany was loved by everyone it seemed, from garbage men to the local doctor. Ryan had never made it clear that he was interested in her, and whenever she would walk to school, he would loiter either a street behind, or a street ahead. He could not even bring himself to talk to the girl. One Valentine's Day he decided to do something to rectify this sorry state of affairs and sent her an expensive, heavily-embroidered, Valentine's card, and unwisely and against tradition, he signed his name on it – his full name.

On the morning of 14 February 1995, Ryan was dreamily drifting along the streets to school, when a beautiful voice behind him asked: "Are you Ryan?"

He spun round. It was Bethany, and she stood with a giant of a boy named Todd. In her hand she held Ryan's unmistakable, old-fashioned-looking Valentine. She was grinning.

"Yep," Ryan replied. He didn't like the way Todd was sneering at him, looking him up and down, no doubt laughing at his clothes, which were not particularly fashionable.

"Well, here's your card back. Todd's my Valentine."

Bethany coldly handed the card back to Ryan, whose heart felt as if it had just been injected with ice.

"Okay," he whispered.

Ryan took hold of the card, folded it and angrily threw it into a litter-bin nearby, as the smug couple walked on. Now all had been revealed to Ryan. Bethany was just a cruel, cold girl who had delighted in mocking his affection for her. He felt no animosity or feelings of revenge towards Bethany and Todd, he was just thankful in a strange way that he had found her out. He knew in his broken heart that there was someone out there who was right for him. He just had to cross her path, that was all.

Well, nothing much romantic happened in Allentown for most of that year. Then, in October, Ryan and his family moved to another part of the town. The new residence was a very old house which dated back to 1900. From the moment Ryan stepped inside the hall, he felt there was something which he could only describe as magical about it. As the weeks went by, Ryan and his family learned from neighbours that the house was allegedly haunted – by a ghostly girl. No one knew the identity of the ghost, or anything about the history of the house, except for an old woman named Eleanor, who was currently in hospital after a fall at her home. Ryan's father reassured his three children that all the talk about ghosts was ridiculous nonsense. He said he had once worked near a graveyard at a factory on nightshifts and had never once seen anything remotely supernatural.

But one evening, one of Ryan's sisters said she could smell a sweet scent in her room, and insisted that she had felt something brush past her that felt like a soft silky veil. Her father dismissively said it had been her imagination. Then Ryan's mother was cooking supper late one evening, waiting for her husband to return from work, when she heard the sounds of a piano playing. Ryan's mother was too frightened to investigate, but she woke up her children and asked them if they could hear the music. They could, and they were a bit spooked too. Ryan loved a challenge, and he took his flashlight and decided to investigate the source of the phantom music. He realised it was coming from upstairs, and so he ascended the staircase, then hesitated outside the attic door. He took a deep breath and pushed the door open. He aimed the beam of the flashlight into the room and swept it about. There was just junk up there, and a large covered object.

The music suddenly stopped. The attic light-bulb was missing, but Ryan walked into the room anyway. He could hear the faint voices of his mother and sisters calling him back but he continued his investigation. He lifted the large canvas dust-sheet off the object, and saw it was an old upright piano. A badly-tuned one, with several dead keys. That could not possibly have been the source of the sweet music he had heard.

Ryan suddenly got the intense feeling he was being watched. It gave him goosebumps, so he backed out of the room, whistling to himself, and closed the door. He went down and told his mother and sisters what he had found.

Suddenly the front door flew open and they all screamed. It was just Ryan's father, home from work.

"What's up? Why are you all standing in the hall?" he laughed, and took off his coat.

His wife told him about the phantom piano player and of the discovery in the attic, but Ryan's dad just shook his head.

"That's just been mice in that old piano," he laughed, trying to sound more convincing than he felt. "Where's my tea? I'm starving."

That night, the first of many visitations took place. Ryan was lying in the ink-black darkness of his bedroom, trying to get to sleep, with the blankets almost over his head to keep out the ghosts, when he noticed the strong scent of lavender. He just knew something was in his room. Then he heard a whisper.

"Ryan ..." it started.

His heart skipped a beat.

"Go away!" he shouted, his voice muffled as he buried his head in the blankets.

The voice was not from either of his sisters playing a prank. He did not recognise it.

"Don't be scared of me, please. My name is Alice," said the voice in the darkness.

"Mom!" Ryan called.

He closed his eyes tightly and threw himself out of bed. He clicked on the light. The room was empty. But the distinctive smell was still lingering.

"Ryan?" came his sister's familiar voice from outside the room. He opened the door and told her about the eerie voice calling itself Alice, and the haunting smell.

"You okay?" she asked gently.

His sister was sympathetic. She too felt there was something supernatural at large in the house.

"I dunno. Yeah, go back to bed," Ryan said.

His sister just nodded, then walked off. She yelled as she bumped into her younger sister, who had come to see what the commotion was about. As Ryan was closing his door, he heard his sister telling her older sister: "The ghost must have visited Ryan."

So Ryan slept with the light on. At 4am he woke up for some reason, then remembered the disembodied girlish voice. Then he felt something warm. He felt a hand holding his. A soft, small hand clasping his outstretched hand, which was dangling out of the bed. Ryan pulled his hand back and held it to his chest. He felt a hot flush in his face and his heart pounded.

"Who's there?" he cried.

No reply came and sleep gradually overtook him as the reassuring pale blue light of dawn crept through the curtains. He had the strangest dream. He met a beautiful, very old-fashioned girl named Alice. She had a pretty impish face, and long, plaited, chestnut-coloured hair. The dream seemed to go on for hours and hours, and in the midst of this misty drama of Ryan's unconscious, there were glimpses of a strange house that stood where Ryan's house was. Stranger still, Ryan was besotted with Alice, and she loved him too. He watched her playing the upright piano he had found in the attic. Then after playing, she whispered to him: "My picture is in this piano. When you wake up, go upstairs and you'll find it."

"When I wake up?" Ryan had replied, dumbfounded, "But I'm not asleep."

"Oh, but you are," Alice told him, and as she kissed him, he awoke.

His heart sank. The dream had seemed so real to him.

At noon, Ryan remembered the dream girl's intriguing claim about her picture being in the piano. He made his way up to the attic. With sunlight from the noonday sun blazing through the skylight, he did not feel in the least afraid. He opened the top flap of the old piano and shone his flashlight into the inner workings of the instrument. There was something down there in the thick mildewed dust, nestling amongst the taut piano wires. Ryan reached down, straining his shoulder until he finally retrieved the object. It was an old framed photograph.

His heart jumped. The girl in that photograph was Alice.

Ryan raced downstairs and showed the photograph to his parents and sisters, and told them about the vivid dreams. Ryan's sceptical father scoffed: "It's all coincidence. If you believe in your dreams you might as well spend your life asleep."

Old Eleanor, the neighbour who could throw some light onto the history of the house, came out of hospital later that week, and was being looked after by her niece. Ryan's mother took a bunch of flowers and a box of chocolates round – and took the photograph out of the piano around too. Eleanor, who was such a sweet old lady, told Ryan's mother.

"That picture will be of Alice Hadley. My mother told me all about her. Alice died of fever in the 1880s. Her mother was very puritanical. Kept the girl from seeing boys and having friends. She used to play the piano. They took the piano out of the house before it was demolished, then after they built the house you're now living in, which stands on the same spot, Alice's piano somehow ended back in there by a fluke. A man named Raymond Jones lived in your house around 1900, and he bought the piano from a store. My mother said it was the very piano Alice used to play. Mr Jones was just a magpie, and he never played that piano, he just had it put away in the attic with the rest of the junk he hoarded."

Ryan's mother was so fascinated that she asked Eleanor if she had heard about the ghost that haunted the house. Eleanor replied, with a glint in her eye, "Yes, and I swear before Almighty God, I saw Alice looking out of the window one day in your home. I hope I'm not scaring you?"

"No, you're not. I'm intrigued," Ryan's mother replied with a smile.

Ryan underwent a peculiar change. He spent most of his days up in the attic, and sometimes his parents would hear beautiful music, even though they both knew their son could not play a note. Ryan would chat at the dinner table about how beautiful and talented Alice was and he chillingly forecast that on the day he died, he would marry her in heaven.

Ryan's father was becoming very concerned about his son's morbid behaviour, and he contacted a local Catholic priest one morning on his way to work. The priest visited the family accompanied by a medium, which infuriated Ryan.

"Mind your own business!" he bawled at the priest. "Alice isn't some evil spirit! She's my girl!"

The priest said it was possible that the boy was becoming "obsessed and possessed with Alice" and recommended a cleansing of the house. Ryan's father consented to this enthusiastically. The procedure took place without Ryan's knowledge whilst he was at school. That evening, when he returned from school, he found a strange silence in the house.

His sisters did not say a word as he came in, and his mother had a strange, sad look in her eyes.

Ryan went straight up to the attic, but came down about fifteen minutes later.

"She's gone!" he choked.

His mother hugged him, as his sisters looked on with morose expressions.

"Alice has gone. I don't understand."

Ryan pushed his mother away.

"The church sent these people ..." his Mom started to say, but trailed off and shook her head. Ryan recoiled.

"What people?"

"They cleansed the house," explained his mother.

"Two psychics carried out a sort of exorcism," added one of his sisters, "and made Alice go into the light."

"And who let them in? You Mom?" Ryan asked, with a disgusted look and tears flowing down his cheeks.

She nodded, "Your Father's idea. He was so worried about you."

"I loved her ..." Ryan sobbed. "I was in love with her. She was all I had and you did this."

He ran up to the attic, shouting behind him for everyone to leave him alone.

The ghost of Alice Hadley never did return. Ryan initially threatened to commit suicide so that he could be reunited with his lost love, but he gradually got over the loss, and later married. He has named one of his children Alice, and strangely enough, that little girl wants to learn how to play the piano.

Mummy's Warning

Around 1956, John Molyneux was thirteen, and he lived with his family in a certain street quite close to Wavertree Playground. I do not wish to identify the street, because there are people living in the house where this strange incident took place.

John had two brothers and three sisters, and one morning he woke up a bit later than usual, at about twenty minutes to nine, and as he rubbed his eyes, he heard his mother shouting him. He yawned and stretched. The room was still a bit dark because the curtains had not been opened

124

yet. John glanced up towards the bedroom door, and saw something that sent a shiver down his spine. A man, about six feet in height, stood there, encased from head to toe in bandages, just like a mummy. John was so terrified, that he could not even shout down to his mother, and he ducked under the blankets. Moments later, he peeped out and found that the bandaged stranger was still there, only this time he was pointing at John.

John heard his mother shouting: "John, you're going to be late for school! Hurry up!"

But the child could not leave the room, because the alarming apparition was blocking his way. As he shouted to his mother, the man swathed in bandages pointed at him again and moved sideways, away from the door. John was paralysed with fear, and he lay there in the gloomy bedroom for so long that his mother and her five other children left the house without him. She set off for work, and the children for school. The echoing slam of the front door meant that John was now all alone in the house.

It was now or never, so he bolted from his bed and ducked under the ghostly mummy's arm. He yanked open the door, and with his heart pounding in his ears, he almost toppled down the stairs and fled out of the front door. He ran as fast as he could to a neighbour's, still in his pyjamas, and although they could see he had had a fright, they did not believe the mummy story.

The boy told anyone who would listen about the weird mummy in his bedroom, but most people just dismissed it as a nightmare. However, a few days later, John Molyneux was fixing himself a snack in the kitchen, when a large kettle full of boiling water was accidentally knocked off the stove. The entire contents splashed all over John, and he screamed out in agony and collapsed. The skin peeled off his back and arms as he was taken to Sefton General Hospital, where he later contracted pneumonia. In those days burns and scalds were not treated with sophisticated, specialised dressings. Instead, they wrapped John Molyneux in bandages from head to foot.

As he lay in the hospital bed, he often wondered about the strange mummy he had seen in his room. It had pointed at him. Had the thing been warning him that he would be the one swathed in bandages next? Perhaps the mummy had been the ghost of a person who had also suffered severe burns in the house where the Molyneuxs had lived, because I have researched the street in Wavertree, and found that in 1902 there was actually a fire in the very house in which John Molyneux saw the mummy.

OTHER TITLES BY TOM SLEMEN

HAUNTED LIVERPOOL 1	Tom Slemen	£5.99
HAUNTED LIVERPOOL 2	Tom Slemen	£5.99
HAUNTED LIVERPOOL 3	Tom Slemen	£5.99
HAUNTED LIVERPOOL 4	Tom Slemen	£5.99
HAUNTED LIVERPOOL 5	Tom Slemen	£5.99
HAUNTED LIVERPOOL 7	Tom Slemen	£5.99
HAUNTED LIVERPOOL 8	Tom Slemen	£5.99
HAUNTED LIVERPOOL 9	Tom Slemen	£5.99
HAUNTED LIVERPOOL 10	Tom Slemen	£5.99
HAUNTED LIVERPOOL 11	Tom Slemen	£5.99
HAUNTED LIVERPOOL 12	Tom Slemen	£5.99
HAUNTED LIVERPOOL 13	Tom Slemen	£5.99
HAUNTED LIVERPOOL ANTHOLOGY	Tom Slemen	£6.99
STRANGE LIVERPOOL	Tom Slemen	£5.99
HAUNTED WIRRAL	Tom Slemen	£5.99
LIVERPOOL GHOST WALK	Tom Slemen	£5.99
HAUNTED CHESHIRE	Tom Slemen	£5.99
WICKED LIVERPOOL	Tom Slemen	£5.99
HAUNTED LIVERPOOL double cassette and audio book read by	Tom Slemen	£8.99

Available from all good bookshops
For a free stocklist contact:
The Bluecoat Press
19 Rodney Street
Liverpool L1 9EF
Telephone: 0151 707 2390
Website: www.bluecoatpress.co.uk

If you have had a paranormal encounter, or a supernatural experience of any
sort, please drop a line to Tom Slemen c/o the above address.